EMPOWER
AND LET GO

Build an amazing team, complex products
and services with Agile Project Management

GERALD O'CONNOR
BA MA MSC PMP PMI-ACP

EMPOWER AND LET GO

Gerald O'Connor

ISBN: 1537102605
ISBN 13: 9781537102603
Library of Congress Control Number: 2016913681
CreateSpace Independent Publishing Platform
North Charleston, South Carolina

A leader is best when people barely know he exists, when his work is done, his aim fulfilled, they will say: we did it ourselves.

—LAO TZU

Contents

Foreword · xvii

Preface · xix

Acknowledgments · xxiii

Accompanying Online Course · · · · · · · · · · · · · · · · · · xxv

Section 1 Agile Project Management ·1

Introduction· ·3

Creating alignment and commitment
by envisioning a clearer future · · · · · · · · · · · · · · · · · ·6

Envisioning and Evolving Products · · · · · · · · · · · · · · 10

Starting an Agile Project—the Visioning Meeting· ·11

The Steps to Creating a Time-Boxed
Agile Project Plan · 16

Velocity and Planning · 18

Agile Strategic Planning—the Release
Planning Meeting · 19

Pressure versus Burnout—the Iteration-Length
Balance · 23

Gathering Requirements by Having
Conversations about User Stories · · · · · · · · · · · · · · · 25

The Agile Race Is Measured in Story Points · · · · · · · · 29

Designing Software For People Using Personas
and Roles · 31

        Roles · 32

The Last Responsible Moment · · · · · · · · · · · · · · · · · 35

The Atomic Level: Tasks · 38

Meetings: Sprint Planning, Sprint Review,
and Retrospectives · 40

        Sprint Planning· 40

        Sprint Review · 41

The Importance of the Daily Stand-Up · · · · · · · · · · · 42

The Chicken and the Pig · 44

The Self-organizing Team and the Role of
the Product Owner · 45

        Role of the Product Owner · · · · · · · · · · · · · · · 46

Agile Project Phases and Phase Gates· · · · · · · · · · · ·47

    Proof of Concept ·47

    Proof of Concept: Minimum Viable Product · · · ·48

    Phase: Explore—Adapt—Implement· · · · · · · · · ·50

    Explore—Adapt—Implement: Release
    Planning Meeting for Release X · · · · · · · · · · · ·50

    Close Phase· ·51

Visibility at a Granular Level:
User-Story Card Template ·53

    Structure of the User-Story Card · · · · · · · · · · · ·54

Visualizing the Project with the Agile Project
Data Sheet ·58

    Product Vision ·59

    Project Objective· ·59

    Business Objective· ·59

    Trade-Off Matrix ·59

    Exploration Factor ·60

    Capability ·60

    Quality Objectives ·60

    Performance Guidelines · · · · · · · · · · · · · · · · · ·61

Major Project Milestones · · · · · · · · · · · · · · · · · 61

Architecture Guideline · · · · · · · · · · · · · · · · · 61

Issues and Risk · 61

Refactoring, Technical Debt, and Slack · · · · · · · · · · 62

Refactoring · 63

Slack · 64

Technical Debt and Pair Programming · · · · · · · · · · 65

Spikes, Tasks, and Bugs · · · · · · · · · · · · · · · · · · 67

Section 2   Metrics, Management and Organization · · · · · · · · · · · · 69

Metrics for Agile Team Performance · · · · · · · · · · · 71

Agile Project Management Reporting and Control · · · 73

Daily Stand-Up Meetings · · · · · · · · · · · · · · · · · 74

Iteration · 75

Epics, Waves, and Releases · · · · · · · · · · · · · · · · 76

Project Charter · 77

Program · 77

Portfolio · 77

Maximizing the Return on Investment in the Project · · 78

Monitoring Application Life Signs with
Test-Driven Development · 80

Organic Risk Management · · · · · · · · · · · · · · · · · · · 83

Schedule Risk · 84

Personnel Risk · 85

Specification Risk · 85

Scope Creep · 86

Empowered Agile Procurement· · · · · · · · · · · · · · · · 87

Agile Human Resources: Turning Good
People into Great Teams· 89

Our Values · 89

Defining the Team's Goals and Values · · · · · · · · · 90

Transitioning from a Type-X Manager to Type-Y· · 90

The Coach · 91

Office Layout: Room to perform · · · · · · · · · · · · · · · 93

An AMO Can Bring Serious Firepower to an
Agile Team · 95

Establishing and Supporting an Agile Culture · · · 96

Providing a Training Program to
All Agile Practitioners · 96

Following Developments in the Agile Industry · · · 96

Bridging the Gap between Senior
Management and Agile Teams · · · · · · · · · · · · · · 97

Defining a common reporting standard
and ensuring compliance · · · · · · · · · · · · · · · · 97

Removing Anything That Hinders
the Performance of an Agile Team · · · · · · · · · · · 97

Co-Ordinating a Pool of Shared Resources · · · · · 98

Agile Management, Coaching, and Responsibility · · · 99

Management · 99

Coaching · 100

1. Educating the Team on the Agile
Method Being Used · · · · · · · · · · · · · · · · · · · 101

2. Focusing the Team on the Highest
Priorities of the Product Owner · · · · · · · · · · · · 101

3. Running Meetings Effectively and
Efficiently in Service of the Team · · · · · · · · · · · 101

4. Removing Barriers that Hinder the Team · · · 101

5. Introducing Engineering Practices and
Adherence (Test-Driven Development,
Continuous Integration, Done-Done Code) · · · · 102

6. Coaching the Team to Peak Performance · · · · 102

Team Values: The Foundation for
High-Performing Teams · 104

Section 3   Learn, Master, and Transcend · · · · · · · · · · · · · · · · · · · 107

Shu-Ha-Ri · 109

"Shu" · 109

"Ha" · 110

"Ri" · 110

Agile Team Energy and Game Theory · · · · · · · · · · · 112

Competitive Element in Software Development · · 113

Individual Sports · 114

Team Sport · 114

Competitive League Environment · · · · · · · · · · · 115

Leadership Is Assumed, Not Assigned · · · · · · · · · · · 117

Great Teams · 118

Self-Organizing Teams · 119

The Superhero Syndrome and the Systems Thinker · · 121

Generative versus Reactive Learning · · · · · · · · · · · 124

Reactive versus Generative Learning · · · · · · · · 125

Feedback Loop · 125

When a Project Is Considered a Failure · · · · · · · · · 126

Section 4   Why Agile? · 129

Empower Your Team with Agile
Project Management · 131

Empowerment · 131

Ownership · 132

Volunteers · 133

The Principles of Agile Project Management · · · 133

You Can't "Plan Away" Uncertainty · · · · · · · · · · · 135

Plan—Do—Adapt · 135

Planning for Change · 137

The Five Themes of Agile Software Development · · · 139

1. Improve the Process · · · · · · · · · · · · · · · · · 139

2. Rely on People · 139

3. Eliminate Waste · 140

4. Deliver Value · 141

5. Seek Technical Excellence · · · · · · · · · · · · · · 142

The Business Argument for Adopting Agile · · · · · · 143

1. Faster Product Adaptability to Market Changes · · 144

2. Continuous Innovation · · · · · · · · · · · · · · · · 144

3. Predictable Results · · · · · · · · · · · · · · · · · · · 145

How Agile Project Management Simplifies
the Constraints of Resources/Time/Functionality · · 147

Time · 147

Cost and Resources · 148

Functionality· 148

Why Agile? Here Is How 3,925 Professionals
Responded · 150

Some Have Failed · 150

An Evolving Industry· 152

Results · 152

Is Agile for Your Team? · · · · · · · · · · · · · · · · · · 153

FOREWORD

I first encountered the "agile" movement in the early 2000s while working with IONA Technologies, the groundbreaking Irish start-up that
led the market in standards-based innovative middleware software.
What impressed me most about the approach was not just the common
sense of the theory involved, but also the speed by which under-pressure
and skeptical software engineers (and their team leaders) not only em-
braced the new approach but became the most ardent advocates of the
approach among their peers in the software industry.

In the mid-2000s, I was not surprised to start to see the approach
being applied beyond software projects. The approach was being used
(with appropriate adaptations) with great success in multidisciplinary
teams, such as those found in the TeleManagement Forum (a nonprofit
industry association for service providers in the telecommunications and
entertainment industries and their suppliers).

As the approach is well-established and well-proven, Trinity College
Dublin has been teaching our undergraduates the theory involved for
a number of years and, more importantly, getting them to live the practices as part of their group software-development projects in second and
third years. This part of their education is consistently highlighted as
being the most valuable upon their return from their fourth-year intern-
ships in a wide variety of industries, with comments such as "I could just
slot into the way the team worked."

In preparation for this foreword, I asked my colleague what he felt the hardest thing about agile project management was. (He lives the agile approach every day with his twenty-strong professional software-development team as part of the ADAPT centre (http://www.adaptcentre.ie) in TCD). His reply was simple: "Getting started!"

Thus I am delighted to introduce Gerald's book, as I believe it not only provides a wonderful basis for someone to adopt agile project management but also provides useful tips and experiences to support existing practitioners.

Prof. Declan O'Sullivan | head of intelligent systems
School of Computer Science and Statistics
Trinity College Dublin

PREFACE

I have managed a wide and diverse range of projects, both in my career and in my free time.

As a professional project manager, and previously as a software developer, I have worked in multinational firms in the telecommunications industry, the public sector, the publishing industry, and the financial sector. In each of these industries, my managers and teams have struggled to find an approach applicable to managing the complexity they faced in typical software projects.

Whether it is a changing market, changing requirements from the customer, changing software, or evolving hardware, there are many moving parts in a software project that make each one completely new and unique. An agile form of management is best-suited under these unique constraints.

There are many approaches and techniques that fall under the banner of agile project management, and, as the old ones evolve, new approaches appear alongside them. What they all share is a set of principles that were originally published in 2001.

http://agilemanifesto.org/

We are uncovering better ways of developing
software by doing it and helping others do it.
Through this work we have come to value:

Individuals and interactions over processes and tools
Working software over comprehensive documentation
Customer collaboration over contract negotiation
Responding to change over following a plan

While there is value in the items on
the right, we value the items on the left more.

In the first section of this book you will be brought through an agile process for managing a project, from establishing the vision to final delivery of the product or service. After you complete this section of the book, you will be prepared to undertake your next project following agile principles.

The second section will look at agile metrics and reporting: how to ensure that your project is kept on track and within schedule.

The third section looks at some principles beyond the current state of agile project management. For example, what role could game theory play in the professional management of project teams? How is a fluid leadership style supported and encouraged in an agile environment? How do you make your team a great team and one that your employees are proud to be a part of?

The final part of this book examines the proposition of why you should adopt these principles as the basis for your next project. My career has not been limited to the software industry; I have also been involved in the running of a newspaper, promoting Broadway shows, and in a number of human-rights projects, and I firmly believe that in many of these cases, an agile approach to the project will deliver the best results.

If you have any feedback on this book or would like to discuss any part of it with me, I would be delighted to hear from you. My e-mail is Gerald@geroconnor.com.

Gerald O'Connor

ACKNOWLEDGMENTS

Thank you to my wife, Wei, for your encouragement and support. Your unwavering belief in my ability has been an endless source of motivation.

This book brings together all the things I have learned and applied in my career and has borrowed heavily from other authors including:

- *Joy, Inc.: How We Built a Workplace People Love,* by Richard Sheridan
- *How to Win Friends & Influence People,* by Dale Carnegie
- *Agile Retrospectives: Making Good Teams Great,* by Esther Derby and Diana Larsen
- *Agile Estimating and Planning,* by Mike Cohn
- *The Art of Agile Development,* by James Shore
- *Agile Software Development: The Cooperative Game,* by Alistair Cockburn
- *User Stories Applied: For Agile Software Development,* by Mike Cohn
- *The Software Project Manager's Bridge to Agility,* by Michele Sliger and Stacia Broderick
- *Coaching Agile Teams,* by Lyssa Adkins
- *Agile Project Management with Scrum,* by Ken Schwaber
- *Agile Project Management: Creating Innovative Products,* by Jim Highsmith
- *Continuous Delivery,* by Jez Humble and David Farley

I highly recommend reading all these books. Everywhere a project is managed with agile guiding principles is different and is shaped by the local unique characteristics. Reading each of these books (including the ones not directly about agile project management) will enrich your reserve of knowledge and will enable you to have a broader mind when encountering issues in your next project.

This book is partially inspired by my mother Rita O'Connor and the success of her book, *In the Rare Auld Times*. Her effort to write her book and get it published over a period of twenty years is a momentous feat of determination and self-belief. My father has also given advice and feedback. Thank you.

Writing a book is a long and arduous process that I was empowered to complete due to my practice of Falun Gong meditation, whose governing principles are truth, compassion, and tolerance.

Finally, thanks to my fellow IT/project-management professionals and friends Martin Murphy and Tom Houston who provided feedback and advice throughout the process. Thanks, lads!

Accompanying Online Course

This book has a complimentary online course, and community, where readers can complete assignments and share their progress and thoughts on agile project management with fellow students.

Sign up at:

www.empowerandletgo.com

SECTION 1
AGILE PROJECT MANAGEMENT

INTRODUCTION

One of the most fundamental desires of human beings is to be seen as being good at something, to be seen among your peers as adding value. Individuals who are empowered to be the best versions of themselves that they can possibly be will surpass not only their own goals and aspirations, but those of management and the team around them.

Many people who arrive at work every morning do so in order to earn a salary, to pay the bills, and to provide a better life for their families. They are professional, and they do a good job, but, at best, they are at 60 percent of their true capacity.

Part of the obstacle that stops individuals from reaching their full professional capacity in organizations is the traditional monitoring and controlling aspect of management.

Staff are managed from the top down, with responsibility and power resting firmly with management. The problem with this approach is that results are limited by the capability of those in management positions. You may have brilliant people in your organization, but if you rely on traditional forms of management, you may be suppressing their innate ability.

Servant leadership is a term that has emerged from the agile project management school of thought. Servant leadership is where the role of the manager on an agile team is to serve the team. The role is to remove anything that blocks the team from doing its work. The role is not to monitor and control but, instead, to manage the agile system of Daily Standups, Retrospectives, and other processes and tools that will empower the team to be highly productive and efficient.

As a team matures, it is possible that it will be completely empowered and be able to manage the agile process itself. As an agile team matures, the role of management decreases, and team members come into their full stride.

There are many different disciplines that have emerged from the "Agile Manifesto" that was originally published in 2001, when seventeen software-development professionals got together to discuss the way that software projects were managed.

Although the meeting was initially focused on software development, the movement that emerged from it and that continues to mature can provide a school of thought for the management of any team trying to achieve any goal.

Managing software teams presents many difficult challenges. First, the IT industry has, since its inception, undergone continual and rapid change. The tools developers use change, the skills they need change, the problems they solve change, and the markets their products are sold into change at an extremely fast pace.

Of course things evolve in other industries too, but, in the software industry, the entire landscape can change drastically during a short period of time.

What makes agile management relative to more industries today is the fact that IT brings high levels of change to all industries, and managers need to be able to handle the changing landscape that faces them.

What makes an agile style of management so compelling is that it takes this complex and challenging set of constraints and creates a fluid environment where the team is empowered to have the best chance of successfully overcoming the challenges that lie in its path.

Many management styles are considered to fall under the agile banner. Scrum, lean, extreme programming, and others mostly fall within the parameters set out in the "Agile Manifesto."

In this book, we will present an agile process from beginning to end, from the conception of a project to its completion. We will examine how to put in place the various agile processes that will help to empower your team. We will examine metrics and control systems that are used to ensure the projects you are working on stay on track and are delivered on time.

We will look outside the box at gamifying a working environment to get better results or at emergent leadership, where different members of the team assume the leadership position at different stages of a project.

We will look at the role willpower or the Superhero Syndrome has in helping a company drive forward in a quickly changing landscape, and how a systems thinker also plays a crucial role in maintaining the integrity of the structure of an organization as it changes. We will look at the powerful role generative learning has in an organization and contrast it with reactive learning.

Most of what is described in this book can be applied to any profession or discipline. If you read the "Agile Manifesto" and thought you would like to try to apply it in your organization, this book will explain how.

CREATING ALIGNMENT AND COMMITMENT BY ENVISIONING A CLEARER FUTURE

T rue empowerment comes from within. One of the most basic human desires is to be seen as being good at something, and it is the responsibility of management to create an environment where staff believe they can be successful. Employees, teams, and companies need to have a clear vision of what perfection looks like to them so that they can work toward it.

Most mature companies have a vision. They have a clear picture of where they want their company to be in five, ten, or twenty years' time. Oxfam's vision is "A just world without poverty." Amazon's vision statement is, "Our vision is to be earth's most customer centric company; to build a place where people can come to find and discover anything they might want to buy online." Although these statements are good and will definitely assist management in ensuring that they are investing their resources in the most strategic place to achieve their vision, will these vision statements really generate a drive from within their employees to be the best version of themselves they can possibly be?

Alignment
A well-defined company vision statement is critical in aligning the company in one direction to realize its vision, but the best you can hope for

is compliance from your staff. In this scenario, your staff understand the mission and vision of the company, and, when they make decisions that affect the company, they will keep them in mind. A clearly defined vision provides a broad road map for direction of staff at all levels of the company. But the most a good company vision statement can generally hope for is compliance, and never commitment. When staff members are at work and getting paid, their actions will comply with management's broader vision for the company, but, on their own time, they will never give it a second thought.

In order to generate commitment and to tap into the internal reserves of drive and energy of staff members, you must help them discover their personal vision statements, and help them align them with the company's. This is where they want to see themselves professionally, personally, and economically in the next five or ten years. If individuals are in careers they like, their personal vision statements should be well-aligned with their careers and company.

Commitment
The benefit of helping the members of your team create a personal vision statement is that it helps them to focus on what they envisage as a future they can commit to working toward. If employees are in careers they like, their vision statements will include aspects of how they see their skills, experiences, and careers developing over the next few years. This vision is personal to each employee. As they look inside to see what drives them, they will inevitably tap into they really want. After creating their personal visions of their futures, you can be sure that when they turn up to work the next day, they will be infused with a new sense of drive and purpose that they didn't bring before. Many won't wait for work to start the next day; they will happily work on their own time to realize their dreams.

After the personal vision statement is complete, management has a role in aligning the company's various training and staff-development resources to help the employees devise plans that they believe will help them realize their visions. Every three months, the manager can sit down with the staff members to help them revise their visions and strategies.

It is important to note that not everyone is ready to define their personal vision statements. Maybe there is too much going on in their lives for them to really think that far into the future. Maybe they are expecting a child or buying a house, and their full focus is on the here and now. If a team member is not ready to engage in the process, it is better to leave it until he or she is. A superficial vision statement is a waste of time and energy.

Team Vision Statement
After all members of the team are given the opportunity to create their own personal vision statements and are supported by the company to devise strategies that they are confident will help them achieve them, then it is time to create the team vision statement.

The team vision statement is the bridge between the company vision statement and the personal vision statements. In order to devise a meaningful team vision, both of these need to be in place first.

In a software company, for example, part of a developer's personal vision statement might be, "I am a software architect who brings best practice in industry to the projects I work on. I give talks in conferences three times a year and am a thought leader in my space." The company that this individual works for has the following vision statement: "Our customers consider themselves part of the team. They feel central to our software-development process. They consider the solutions we build their solutions."

In this company, there might be a team that focuses on building mobile applications for customers. Their vision statement may be, "Our team are committed to being the best in industry in our field. We are committed to bringing the best techniques in the mobile-development industry to our customers and to exceeding their expectations and imaginations."

In the above example, you can easily see how the alignment down to the staff on the floor will create an environment where team members are focused and committed to realizing their visions, both on their own time and on company time.

Personal vision and team vision statements lead to company alignment and commitment from individuals. Personal visions are the foundations to empowering individuals to become the best versions of themselves that they can possibly imagine.

ENVISIONING AND EVOLVING PRODUCTS

The empires of the future are empires of the mind.
—WINSTON CHURCHILL

Some projects only need resources and a plan. The plan may have been completed one hundred times before, and it is pretty certain that following the same plan will deliver a similar result. The smallest details can be predicted because of experience with previous similar projects.

More complex projects however start with a high-level vision. One has to imagine what the product may look like when finished because there are no examples to follow. The vision is the highest level of abstraction for a project. From the vision, the product evolves.

An agile project evolves by starting from the vision statement and deciding what the major themes that may exist in the product are. Then take the most important of these themes and break it down into user stories. Then prioritize the user stories into the product backlog, and, finally, implement the top user story on the list.

As you keep implementing the most important thing on the list (product backlog), the project may develop in ways you never thought of at the start. Maybe new technology emerges during the process that changes how we viewed things. Maybe the market the product was to be released into changes. Maybe, if we are releasing the product to customers in iterations, they decide to take the product in an unanticipated direction.

Not only does an agile project management process allow you to manage a complex project when many of the things under your feet are shifting, it also has fundamental values to guide your decision-making process when you come to a fork in the road.

For example, delivering value over meeting constraints. The product owner is at the center of the agile process and has ownership of the prioritized product backlog. This means that while accepting that complex projects may bring up unanticipated events, it is the role of the product owner to decide, based on the information presented by the team, what the best decision is. It is the role of the agile project manager to ensure that value is delivered to the product owner and, at the end of the day, the customer who will use the product.

> *Vision without execution is hallucination.*
> —THOMAS EDISON

If you can predict the outcome of a project because it has been based on plans of similar projects in the past, then it can be built using a process of anticipation (i.e., define, design, and build). You know what is going to happen, so you can anticipate it from the start. If a similar project has not been completed in the past and you cannot accurately anticipate what is going to happen, then you need a fluid process that enables you to adapt to a changing set of variables (i.e., envision, execute, explore, and refine). This is the agile process.

Starting an Agile Project—the Visioning Meeting

> *Vision is the art of seeing what is invisible to others.*
> —JONATHAN SWIFT

An agile project starts with two processes, a visioning meeting and a release planning/backlog-creation meeting.

The purpose of the visioning meeting is to draw up the project charter. Even in agile project management, this document is necessary to think through all aspects of the project in order to make a considered decision on whether or not to implement commission the project.

One of the principles of agile project management is, "Simplicity—the art of maximizing the amount of work not done—is essential." This is true for all aspects of agile project management. Figuring out what to leave out presents a challenge. But thinking things through from this angle ensures that only the most important things get valuable resources.

For the visioning meeting, the people you need present at the meeting are those who have the expertise to create a vision for all aspects of the project. They include

- the product owner;
- stakeholders;
- field experts—technical, marketing, and business, as needed; and
- the project manager.

The product owner needs to be present because this is who owns the end product. This is the person who wants to see the project completed, who sees a burning business need, and who has at least a partial vision of what the product might look like.

Often there are stakeholders behind the scenes who have strong influences on a project getting the green light. There may be some tangential reason why they want the project completed, and this reason may be the driving factor behind why it gets the green light. Agile project management empowers those who use it, and, when you have people who have a passionate interest in seeing a project completed, you should include them in the process.

Experts are important so that decision makers can best understand the market, the technical issues, and the costs. Having a clear view of these factors is central to creating a project charter on which a decision can be made whether to proceed with the project. These experts may have some hard truths to contribute that make a project unattractive to all stakeholders but that are necessary to make an informed decision.

The project manager needs to be present because that is who will create the project charter, chair the meeting, and manage the project.

The project charter consists of the following characteristics:

- product vision
- business need/impact
- high-level requirements/major deliverables
- duration
- cost estimate
- human resources
- stakeholder registry

The product visioning meeting starts with having everyone present create a vision about what the project will look like when it is completed. What impact will the project create? What savings or new income channels will it create? What markets will it open up? What is the overall picture of what the product will look like at completion?

This meeting is led by the product owner, facilitated by the project manager, while drawing upon expert feedback from all in the room.

The next part of the meeting is to draw up the high-level requirements and major deliverables for the project. These are the major aspects of the project when delivery of the project will be considered success. These will become the starting point for creating the product backlog. These major deliverables will be created as a prioritized list, ensuring that the most important things are completed first. It is possible that the major deliverables will change as the project evolves. However, because these deliverables are set at a high level, they will often all be implemented according to the high-level plan, but the details will be handled during the day-to-day management of a project.

The next things to consider are the human-resource needs to carry out the project. What expertise is needed? What type of relevant customers need to be included on the team, and are they available? Are key stakeholders available? Can the product owner make the necessary commitment? The key members of the agile team will remain part of the team for the whole project and may take on different roles in the process at different stages.

When the duration and human resources have been decided, the major deliverables will need to be re-examined, taking these constraints into consideration. Although the list of major deliverables may remain the same, the probability of the lowest-priority deliverables have of being completed may become apparent. Some lower-priority items may be dropped from the high-level plan if enough resources are not made available to complete them.

A stakeholder register needs to be created as part of creating the project charter. Who has an interest in the project and needs to be kept informed of developments? New projects often bring a level of excitement and engagement from those who have tangential interests, and their input can be invaluable to the success of the project. Successfully keeping people engaged in the project can create champions for it throughout the organization. People like to be listened to and feel like their expert input is valued. There will be different levels of stakeholders and different forms of engagement with them.

The final part of the visioning meeting is brainstorming risks, assumptions, and constraints. The initial part of the meeting will opened the groups up to thinking about different aspects of the project and will enable them to flesh out these details. After they have written them down, they can again visit the major deliverables, human resources, and the duration to judge if they are still viable, all things considered.

This meeting should take, at most, four hours.

The purpose of the project charter is to gather the needed information so that the project sponsor can decide whether to proceed with the project and invest the necessary resources. Like all documentation, it will be out-of-date as soon as the ink dries, so it can be thought of as a signpost pointing in the direction the project is most likely to take.

After the project is approved by the project sponsor, the release planning/backlog-creation meeting can be scheduled.

Vision meeting agenda

- executive welcome (project sponsor or champion)
- introduction, ground rules, and review of agenda (project manager)
- What is the goal of this meeting? What is the scope of authority, and what is the motivation for everyone in the room? (Project manager, project sponsor)
- What is the vision for the product? What will the result look like? What business need is this filling? What will be the impact on future business after it is complete? (Product owner)
- What are the major features that will appear on the product road map? (Product owner)
- When does it need to be completed? (Project sponsor)
- How much will it cost? (Project manager)
- Who do we need on the team? (Project Manager)
- Who do we need to keep informed? (Project manager)

THE STEPS TO CREATING A TIME-BOXED AGILE PROJECT PLAN

I t is important in agile project planning to have a clear definition of what the product you are building should look like at the end of the project. You need a vision. The project charter is where you package this vision in order to get the sign-off from the sponsor.

The project charter also outlines all the high-level risks, assumptions, and requirements that are necessary to ensure the project has the best chance of satisfying the sponsor and stakeholders.

There are two types of broad, high-level project plans:

- Time-Boxed Plan. This is where there is a definite deadline, and you need to satisfy the overall vision in order for the project to be a success. During the timeline, you implement as many features as possible from a prioritized product backlog.
- Feature-Boxed Plan. This is where the timeline is open-ended, and the requirement is to implement X number of features during the project.

It is easy to imagine the different scenarios where either of these types of plans could be deemed more appropriate and lead to good results. However, under no circumstances should you ever agree to a time-boxed plan with fixed features. It will seldom work, and either features or the deadline will not be delivered upon.

So you have created the project plan, and you have a hard deadline. The next step is to brainstorm user stories. What are the types of things the user needs this product to do to satisfy the overall vision? Involve as many stakeholders, members of the team, and customers as possible to exhaust every possible scenario.

The next thing is to turn the group of user stories into a prioritized list of items (product backlog) that will be implemented in order, starting with the most important.

It is impossible to accurately define how long a user story will take at this point, because there are too many variables. What you can do is estimate the size of a story relative to the others. Start with the smallest user story, and estimate the size of the others relative to this. Create five drums, and use the numbers one, two, three, five, and eight (the Fibonacci series), where one represents the smallest user case, and the others are multiples of that. Do this for the first twenty user stories in the product backlog. Then go back to the sponsor and ask he or she is still happy with the product-backlog priority list. If not, reorder it.

When you have placed all the user stories into the 5 drums, then for example, you might have 3 in Drum Size 1, 20 in Drum size 2, 4 in Drum Size 3, 6 in Drum Size 5, and 2 in Drum Size 8. The stories in Drum Size 8, are eight times the size of stories in Drum Size 1, The stories in Drum Size 2 are a quarter of the size of the stories in Drum Size 8. It is very difficult to estimate in exact lengths of time in project management, but sizing in multiples is much easier to do, and when the project starts this type of estimating can help determine the velocity of the project, and therefore how long it will take.

Always try to have three iterations (development cycles) of user stories ready.

Velocity and Planning

Generally, it is best to have an iteration every two weeks and a release once a month. These are easy dates for stakeholders to remember. It is impossible to estimate velocity until you have completed at least four iterations. Then you can get an idea of how many user stories where completed during an iteration. Only include stories that are completely finished. Completely finished and in the hands of the customer.

Once you can determine the velocity of the project team, you can give rough estimates to management at planning meetings of when various features will be implemented. These estimates should be given at release demo/ planning meetings.

Using this broad structure, continue to implement and release features until you reach the firm time-boxed deadline for the project. This approach should lead to a satisfactory result for the stakeholders as they will have been able to have influence over and control of the resources of the project in realizing the vision outlined in the project charter.

Agile Strategic Planning—The Release Planning Meeting

You have to be fast on your feet and
adaptive or else a strategy is useless.
—Charles De Gaulle

S trategic plans generally apply over a longer period of time and over a higher level of abstraction. In a company, this means that strategic plans point the direction for a lot of people and resources and point the direction into the medium- and long-term.

This is not to be confused with tactical planning. Tactical planning involves how to manage resources to achieve an immediate, short-term goal.

In World War II, it was a strategic decision to liberate France by the Allies as part of broader and longer Western-front attack. However, the exact approach to how the five-mile stretch of Normandy coast was taken was tactical, short-term, and immediate.

In agile project management, the release planning meeting is where the strategic decisions are made for the project. These are the high-level, long-term deliverables that you decide the project needs to create.

Often these deliverables are measured in relative terms because it is difficult to put exact schedules against them at this point. These deliverables are measured in story points.

The way this is done is as follows. First, decide all the major deliverables. Then you pick which is the smallest. This is one story point. Then you measure the relative size of the others using a multiplier like the Fibonacci series (1, 2, 3, 5, 8, 13, 21, 34). This will give a broad idea of how big each item is relative to another.

The next step is to determine the priority queue for the major deliverables that will make up the road map. What should happen first, second, third, and so forth needs to be decided.

It is important to have all the necessary technical team members and customers (those who will use the product) present to help make this decision.

Technical experts may advise that it is important (cheaper/quicker) for certain technical components to be built first. Marketing experts (customers) may advise that they are waiting to see what their competitors are doing, so they may prefer to delay certain features, or they may wish to raise the priority of some to grab the competitive advantage. Therefore, it is important to have the right people in the room to help make these decisions.

Experts help to guide the decision-making process, but the product owner owns the release plan.

Major deliverables are often at the epic scale. Epics are collections of user stories. Epics can be implemented over a release cycle, but user stories are implemented over an iteration. Iterations are typically a minimum of one week, up to a maximum of two months, in length.

The size of an iteration depends on a number of factors. One is the length of time the largest user story will take, because all stories need to be completed within an iteration. The second thing to consider is how frequently the product owner will want to change the product backlog (order of stories). If changes are frequent, you will need to shorten the iteration because changes cannot be made during an iteration.

Iterations are where tactical decisions are made. Exactly what technical approach is used to implement a feature? What practices are used to ensure quality? What structures are used to help the team perform to the highest standard? These things are of less concern to the product owner or sponsor who just want to see it working as they described.

In agile project management, the plans are living and breathing things that can change. They are not fixed and static. After each iteration, the product backlog should be reviewed with the product owner and the release plan should also be reviewed to ensure that everything is on track and to allow for any new information to be taken into account or changes to be made.

The release plan is a high-level list of major deliverables, and the product backlog is the list of smaller user stories that will be implemented in individual iterations.

During the release planning meeting, last responsible moments need to be clearly indicated. The last responsible moment is a moment in time where if a decision isn't made, it will have a negative impact on the project. Leaving the decision as long as possible means more information is available to make a more-informed decision. For example, if a system needs a database, it may not be necessary to decide the type until it is time to start designing it. This will allow other decisions to be made first that can contribute information to ensure the correct database is chosen when the time comes.

When teams are not collocated, it is important that they try to be present in person for the release planning meeting. They may have some pertinent information to add that will help ensure things are prioritized and scheduled correctly. This is a one-off meeting that sets the direction for the whole project; it is the roadmap that everyone on the project will follow. People can attend remotely, but the effect will not be as good.

Agenda for a release planning meeting

- Introduction, ground rules, purpose, and agenda (project manager)
- Distribution of the project charter. Does anything need to change? Any new information? (product owner)
- What are the major deliverables, and how many story points to do each of them have? (product owner, with the help of the team)
- What are the priorities of the major deliverables or epics? (product owner)
- What is the end date, and can all the deliverables be achieved? (project manager and team)
- What are the release cycle lengths and iteration lengths? (project manager)
- What major deliverables (epics) go into each release? (What is the theme of the release?) (product owner)
- What are the assumptions we are making and the constraints we are dealing with? (project manager)
- What are the last responsible moments for the project? (project manager)
- Can the team commit to this plan? (Everyone signs off.)

PRESSURE VERSUS BURNOUT—THE ITERATION-LENGTH BALANCE

P arkinson's Law is the adage, "Work expands so as to fill the time available for its completion." The iteration length for an agile team is a balance of having enough pressure to ensure the highest level of productivity while avoiding burning out the team.

Following an agile process embraces the fact that software projects have a huge amount of uncertainty and change, and so it adopts short, well-structured, regular meetings.

What's the point of an iteration? An iteration is an interval during which the team produces shippable product. It is the interval in which the team delivers new working features to the product owner. It is the time when you inform all stakeholders of progress. It is the time when you reset your priorities and reflect on the previous iteration.

So how do you define the perfect iteration length? The following factors need to be taken into account:

1. how complex the product is, and how frequently features can be delivered
2. how available stakeholders are for the meetings
3. the balance between the time taken for a retrospective and planning meeting and whether that investment in time is profitable

4. How long it takes for the average user story to be implemented——the iteration length should give enough time to complete most of the user stories

The iteration length acts as the heartbeat of the project. Like every agile technique, it needs to be structured to meet the needs of the project, team, and organization. However, once the best structure is found, it needs to be followed rigidly to provide the stability the team needs to reach its highest levels of productivity.

The two most common iteration lengths for a software product are two weeks and four weeks.

There are some variations on this, like the 6*2+1 structure. This is three two-week iterations of work, and then one week where the team prioritizes tasks itself. This gives the team a chance to tidy up the things it knows must be done, but that might not be seen as a priority by the product owner. This extra week is like a release valve for the team to take the pressure off. It's a great idea.

GATHERING REQUIREMENTS BY HAVING CONVERSATIONS ABOUT USER STORIES

The best ideas start as conversations.
—JONATHAN IVE

Generally people don't get uptight when they hear they are about to have a conversation. Conversations are easy. They aren't overly formal and don't tie you down to long-term commitments. Conversations are generally open-ended, and the details can be discussed again in the future if need be.

User stories are discussions about what particular parts of a project will need to do, based on the current understanding of the problem at hand. They are stories told by the customer about problems that the customer sees the new software solving. They are told by the customer from the customer's point of view.

The customer in this case is the person who will use the software when it is written to solve the problem in question. It is important that the customer writes the user story as that is who understands it best. However, the customer writes it while working with the team of developers, testers, and so on, so that they fully understand what the problem is and can give feedback to the customer about how it might be done.

One way to write a user story is as follows:

I, as a (role), want (function) so that (business value).

This is taken from *User Stories Applied* by Mike Cohn.

The role in the above example is the definition of a particular type of person who will be using the system. The function is what the person actually wants to do and the business value is why he or she wants to do it.

After we have written the definition of the user story, we flesh out the details. It is important to note that, at this point, we are exploring the problem for planning purposes, and we will revisit it in detail when it reaches the top of our product backlog. We want to get as good an understanding of the problem as we can for planning purposes.

The details for the story should be limited to the main bullet points, and they should be written on an index card by the customer. The saying that the customer is always right is relevant here, because the customer will be the one using the software, so it is imperative that the customer writes the definition of the problem.

These bullet points are really reminders of the discussion about the story. They will be revisited when it is time for implementation.

After the broad details of the user story have been documented, the team turns the conversation to tests that, if satisfied, will mean the user story has been implemented correctly and is complete. This is the starting point for the user-acceptance testing. This, too, is just a conversation at this point, and can be revisited later in the process. The tests can be written on the back of the index card.

User stories are not seen as documented requirements in the traditional sense. They are not hard and firm contracts that will be taken out in the future to ensure neither side changes what they agreed to.

Rather than being contracts that documents the user requirement, they are seen as records of conversations that represent how the problem was understood at the time. There is an understanding that they may change in the future and there will not be a penalty for doing so.

There are a number of characteristics that determine a good user story[1]. First, they need to be independent. This is important from a planning point of view. Each user story needs to be implementable without depending on another user story. If it isn't, it becomes difficult to determine when the story is actually done-done.

Stories need to be negotiable. Traditional software-development requirements gathering techniques were black-and-white: "The software shall…" This left no room for misunderstanding and also made it more difficult for the requirement to be refined or discussed further when it came to implementation. User stories are about starting a conversation and having enough information at each stage of the process to make the best decisions for the project. An important principle in agile software development is being able to leave things to the last responsible moment. This often means leaving room so that the details can be negotiated at the last responsible moment before implementation.

User stories are written by the customer because the software is written for the customer. It is the customer who will use it day in and day out. Job satisfaction for the development team comes from seeing all the features it implemented being used regularly because the people who specced them are the people who use them. User stories must be valuable to the customer.

Constraints are not user stories. User stories must be estimable. Constraints may apply broadly to all user stories or a section of them. For example, a constraint may be that a search query returns results in less than one second.

---

1 Mike Cohn, *User Stories Applied: For Agile Software Development* (Pearson Education). Kindle Edition.

When a user story is complete, it needs to be testable. The tests written on the back of the user-story index card are used to demonstrate when the story is fully implemented.

Finally, user stories need to be small. The smallest user story should generally take one developer day to implement, and the largest takes a full iteration. Any bigger than that, and they should be broken up into smaller stories. Any smaller, and perhaps they could be grouped together into a package.

THE AGILE RACE IS MEASURED IN STORY POINTS

I n a traditional race, you know the distance and are pretty sure about the terrain. The challenge is, how fast can you complete it? In an agile software iteration, the number of resources is generally fixed and so is the amount of time, so it becomes a race to complete story points.

What is a story point? If you are working on a new project, the first thing you need to do in agile project management is break down the project into as many user stories as possible. A user story is a scenario that a user goes through to achieve a result. In a shopping-till application the user story might be, "Customer pays for product in order to complete purchase."

For a large project, you may have hundreds of user stories at the end of the requirements-gathering stage. A story point is a relative measure of one user story to another. After you have determined the user stories in a story, look for the smallest one. This story will be one story point.

A story-point estimate is an amalgamation of the amount of effort involved in developing the feature, the complexity of developing it, and the risk inherent in it.

A story point is a relative measure of the size of a user story. If one user story has one story point and the next has two, then the second one is twice the size of the first.

It is a good idea to put user stories into story-point bins of sizes like 1, 2, 3, 5, 8. This is called the Fibonacci series, and it is generally a good scale to use. If a user story does not fit in one bin, then round it up to the next one.

For larger stories you may use a scale like 13, 20, 40, 100. It is important to note that there is a huge amount of uncertainty at this stage in the planning process, so you are not looking to estimate the exact size but rather the size in relation to other user stories in the project.

Once the project starts progressing and user stories are implemented, there is a strong urge to change the estimates for the user stories. Maybe you discover that a user story is more complex, or perhaps less, than initially thought. It is important to not change the original estimate, as the stories were estimated relative to each other, and, over time, the estimates will balance out, and your team will uncover a stable velocity based on the original estimate.

How is the velocity of the team measured? The velocity of the team can be measured once a few iterations of the project cycle have been completed. It is simply measured as the number of story points that have been completed per iteration. This gives an indicator of about how many will be completed in the future and can be planned against.

DESIGNING SOFTWARE FOR PEOPLE USING PERSONAS AND ROLES

If you work just for money, you'll never make it,
but if you love what you're doing and you always
put the customer first, success will be yours.
—RAY KROC

The first principle in the agile manifesto is, "Our highest priority is to satisfy the customer through early and continuous delivery of valuable software."

The customer is at the center of the agile process. The software is built for the customer with the customer actively participating in the process.

However, for some software, there is a multitude of customers. For an online software like Facebook, there are a billion customers. How on earth could you include all of them in the software development process?

The answer is, you can't. But you can try to think from the largest customer group's point of view using a structured process.

Roles

Roles in software development allow us to define a group of people and how they might behave. The roles you will want to consider in a project are those that will use the software or somehow be impacted by it.

Some characteristics of roles that you would want to consider include

- frequency of use of the software;
- features of the software they are likely to use;
- familiarity with computer applications in general;
- the parts of the business process that these roles are involved in; and
- the authority of the role and the impact it has on the perception of the software.

There are potentially a multitude of characteristics to consider when defining roles, many of which may be specific to the application being built.

A good method for discovering roles is to sit down with a broad group of customers and ask them to throw out as many customer roles as they can think of. Make a note of all of them no matter how similar they might be. Write the roles on index cards along with a few characteristics and put them on the table.

If the process is slowing down, pick up one of the roles and ask the person who created it to describe it, and then ask everyone to think of similar or tangential roles.

Continue this process until you think you have a broad section of roles that might use the software.

Place them all on the table and draw connections between them. Discuss which are similar and which can be removed without making the group of roles less representative.

New roles can be added at any point in the process. Some roles may only become clear as the hierarchy and connections between the roles becomes clear.

These roles will be used in the process of defining user stories, which is effectively the definition of what the software does.

User stories can be defined using a template like:

[Role] wants to do [function] in order to achieve [business value].

After the full hierarchy of roles has been created, it can be documented and will be used later in the process of creating user stories.

It is important to flesh out the roles of those who will use the software the most one step more into personas.

A persona is the personification of a particular role.

The process of fleshing out personas involves turning the roles into real people that one can picture. You can picture them coming to work and sitting down to use the software.

This might involve thinking about the following:

- what function they play in the company
- what age they are
- how many children they have
- what cars they drive
- how comfortable they are with computers
- what else they use computers for
- what their days look like
- who they go to lunch with
- who in the office influences them
- what they do in their free time

After you have fully explored the roles and defined all their characteristics, give them names. When you build your user stories, it will be easier for you to think from these personas' perspectives if you can relate to them.

This process is important if you don't have easy access to this type of role during the software-development process because instead of thinking from the perspective of building features to complete a task, you will be thinking of building features that enable the personas to complete some part of their daily jobs that makes life easier for them.

Defining roles and personas are crucial steps in creating software that is designed with the end user in mind. This process ensures that the most important person, the customer, is always at the center of the process.

THE LAST RESPONSIBLE MOMENT

I magine you are Robin Hood. The apple is sitting on the fair maiden's head. She stands one hundred meters away. If you hit the target, you can both walk free. It would be much better for both of you if you could move the target closer, right? Fifty meters closer, ninety meters closer would substantially increase your chances of success. That's what the principle of the last responsible moment means, delaying making a decision until the target is as close as possible. Of course you don't want to wait too long, or the opportunity might be missed.

In software development, there are often one million and one variables that gradually become fixed during the process, making it, at the beginning, extremely difficult to hit the target. Using a traditional waterfall-lifecycle methodology for software management, that is exactly what managers would try to do. They would try to build a detailed plan of everything that needed to be done to complete a project and deliver the beautifully constructed plan to management for approval.

Management would woo and awe over the lovely charts and graphs and be excited at the prospect of completing this great new project.

But when you start, you find that a key hire takes longer than expected. The market changes, and now the scope of the product will be scaled back. New technology emerges that should be adopted. Halfway through, the business users realize a better way of doing things. The initial plan quickly turns null and void; however senior management will still take it out of the drawer and bash you over the head with it when things go off-target.

The last responsible moment is when you avoid making a commitment to a solution to a problem as late as possible, and, by doing so, many of the variables become fixed.

As the project progresses, you gain more information about the following:

- The team: if your team is newly formed, you won't know what it can do. You won't know what velocity it can consistently produce or that management can plan against. Without knowing this information, it is impossible to plan too far into the future.
- The business problem: as the software is incrementally developed, the business users will get a clearer idea on what it is going to look like, and they may want changes. This is inevitable as they will have a vague idea, at most, initially as to what the product will look like when it is finished.
- Infrastructure: in agile software development projects, the infrastructure is developed incrementally. This is so that you don't spend a lot of money building something that won't be used or that may change. By delaying a decision, more of the infrastructure that the tool is built on will be in place. This infrastructure will frame many of the choices that are available for the product. Having more infrastructure in place means better decisions will be made.
- The market: sometimes the market can shift overnight, and sometimes in weeks, months, or years. Any of these time frames can have a major impact on a project or on a product being built. Agile software development allows everyone to keep their fingers on the pulse of the project and can enable it to change direction with a changing market. Delaying a decision as late as possible may enable the project to capitalize on a change in the market place.

Making decisions too early means you will be adding more rework later down the pipeline. Overall, delaying a decision to the last responsible moment means there is less of a chance of that current decisions will be invalidated by later decisions. The cost of delaying the details of a decision as late as possible means it is not possible to create a beautiful Ghant chart at the start of the project that will clearly show how all resources will be used, which is a good thing because they are seldom, if ever, accurate.

THE ATOMIC LEVEL: TASKS

We cannot perform our tasks to the best of our power,
unless we think well of our own capacity.
—WILLIAM GODWIN

I n agile projects, the most granular level of work unit recorded is a task.

User stories are broken down into tasks during the iteration planning meeting. This is an important part of the process because it is possible that a large user story will run the course of the iteration, and the project manager needs to know that the iteration is on track.

It is the responsibility of the team members to break down a user story into tasks. The reason this job is assigned to members of the team rather than the project manager or the product owner is because they have the expertise and know what is involved in building the user story.

The team then self-organizes the tasks involved to complete the user story, sharing the work among the members.

Reporting of the progress for tasks is done during the daily stand-up meetings. During these meetings, members of the team individually report on what they did yesterday, what they will do today, and what problems they encountered. During this meeting, it is possible for the project manager to record what tasks have been completed and whether the team is on track.

A tasks burn-down chart is often used to ensure that the team is on track to complete the iteration on time. Iterations are composed of the user stories that the team made a commitment to complete at the iteration planning meeting.

During an iteration, it is often a good idea to leave buffer time of 25 percent for refactoring or learning. If the team is struggling to make good on its commitments, this buffer can be used to catch up on outstanding tasks. If the team is on track, this is important time for the team to learn or do other tasks that benefit the project but are not directly on the product backlog.

The measurement for tasks is in hours. Tasks are generally at a granular level, so they are much easier to estimate than user stories. The team generally understands the exact details of tasks, so estimates are more accurate.

Finally, tasks don't need to be reported as done-done during a stand-up meeting. They just need to be reported as finished. This is because tasks, by their nature as components of user stories, cannot be said to be completely finished until the complete user story has been finished, tested, demo'ed and released. This inherently means it is possible that tasks may need to be reworked even after they are reported as finished, but hopefully that won't happen too often.

MEETINGS: SPRINT PLANNING, SPRINT REVIEW, AND RETROSPECTIVES

Communication is important for an efficient team, and that means regular meetings. In the agile methodology, it is important that the meetings stick to their defined structure in order to get the best results.

In many companies, when staff members hear that they must go to a meeting, they roll their eyes. They would much prefer to be doing "real" work. It is important that it is clear what the objective of each meeting is, that only the people who need to be there attend, and that it contributes to the success of the project.

In an agile project, there are many types of meetings, including the daily stand-up, sprint planning, sprint review, and retrospectives. Retrospectives are an important part of the agile methodology, and we will discuss them in detail in other sections. But in general, they are opportunities for the team to internally reflect on the last iteration. Agile retrospectives focus on teamwork, the methods of the team, and how to improve them. In this section, we will give an over view of Sprint Planning and Sprint Review.

Sprint Planning

The sprint planning meeting is often broken into two parts. One is where the team meets with the stakeholders and product owner to discuss the priority of user stories in the product backlog. The team also uses this meeting to share with the stakeholders what new things have been learned so the stakeholders have the latest information on hand to make their decisions. On the flip side, the stakeholders and product owner may come with new market information, a new company strategy, or other information that may change the order of the product backlog. The objective of this meeting is to finalize the order of the product backlog for the next iteration.

The second sprint planning meeting is an internal one for the team. During this meeting, the team looks at the highest priorities on the product backlog and decides how many it can commit to for the next iteration. The goal for the iteration is a team decision, and the commitment is a group one. This is important so that there is group accountability at the end of the iteration. At the end of this meeting, the group will have committed to a number of user stories, and, on average, the number of story points will be the same as the velocity for the team. (The velocity is the average number of story points that have been completed per iteration so far. It is an indicator of when user stories on the product backlog will be completed.)

Sprint Review

The sprint review meeting is where the team presents to stakeholders what has been developed during the sprint. These are finished, tested, and released features that have been crossed off the product backlog. These features can now be introduced to customers, and the sales teams can now use them in their pitches. These features will be the features that the stakeholders prioritized as the highest priorities in the last sprint planning meeting, so they will be delighted to see their highest-value features made available.

The Importance of the Daily Stand-Up

H aving a Daily Stand-Up is a core concept of many Agile project management schools of thought, but many software teams who do not employ an agile methodology are confident that weekly meetings are enough, and any more are a waste of time. So who is right?

It depends on how you structure your daily meeting. It is vitally important to stick to a rigid structure and time scale according to best practice.

A Daily Stand-Up meeting is typically fifteen minutes long, and the team has a maximum of eight members. Each is given a couple of minutes to answer three questions:

- What did I do yesterday?
- What will I do today?
- And what problems did I encounter when I was doing the task?

What is the significance of these questions? They are about building a team ethic. In agile projects, the team builds the product, not the individual. Team performance is most important, not the individual. So if a team member needs support and others can help, these questions help to highlight the problem and possibly get support from the team.

The purpose of the meeting is not to start a discussion on a particular problem; no, that could take hours. The purpose is to give every team member a chance to answer the three questions, and further discussion can happen after the Daily Stand-Up.

A second purpose of the meeting is accountability. You say you will get something done today, and you say it in front of your teammates, and tomorrow you will have to answer for whether or not you actually got it done. You won't want to let people down. A daily iteration ensures that everyone knows what everyone else is working on, and problems are solved quickly.

It is not for everyone though. If someone is struggling to keep up with the pace of the team, it will quickly be apparent, and that person will be uncomfortable in this environment in the long-term.

People from other departments may sometimes drop into scrum meetings. It is an essential rule of a scrum meeting that these people cannot talk during the meeting and that they must stand at the edge of the room. This ensures that you can keep the structure of the meeting and the time frame and achieve its objective. If there are questions afterward for any of the team members, they will happily oblige.

THE CHICKEN AND THE PIG

I n project-management, team members are sometimes called pigs, and nonteam members are called chickens. Don't be offended! There is an old parable that explains the labels.

As the story goes, the chicken and the pig were going to set up a restaurant and were discussing what to call it. The chicken said, "Ham'n Eggs," but the pig said, "No, I'd be committed, but you would only be involved."

How does this relate to agile project management? In the daily sand-up, only members of the team can talk and contribute (pigs). Pigs are committed to the project 100 percent. Onlookers, even if they are senior management, cannot talk during the daily stand-up or get involved at all. They can only sit and observe (chickens). After the meeting, they can arrange a separate meeting if they want.

Chickens also do not sit at the meeting-room table. They must sit at the edge of the room or, preferably, stand. This makes their role in the meeting as observers and not participants clear.

It is important to follow these rules as no one likes a long, boring meeting, and attendance will drop if you lose control of the structure of the meeting.

THE SELF-ORGANIZING TEAM AND THE ROLE OF THE PRODUCT OWNER

A t the core of the agile project management is the team, and when the team is looking at tackling a project, it self-organizes to solve the problems it is faced with.

When the team is looking at the product backlog, it does an analysis of the highest-priority user stories, and estimates how many it can complete in the next iteration. It then sets its goals and makes a commitment. This commitment is made as a team, and everyone is involved in the process.

For the team, there are no titles like database expert, or GUI design engineer. Everyone has one title: engineer. The team members will know who has the greater strengths and who they can ask for help when they are stuck with a problem. However, if the database expert is free and there is GUI design to be done, he or she will jump in and do it. Or if a database query needs to be rewritten and the middleware expert is the only engineer free to write it, he or she will jump in and write the query. Over all, it is a team effort in an agile project.

In an agile team, no one outside the team can commit the team to a goal. Only the team itself can manage its workload and make commitments on behalf of the team. This is often difficult for management to get accustomed to. The team is accorded full authority to do whatever it decides is necessary to achieve its goal.

If you have ever played on a sports team, you will know that not everyone plays well all the time. When a member of the team is having a subpar day, then the rest of the team needs to shoulder more of the work. Someone who is continuously underperforming can be removed from the team. Removing someone from the team should be a last resort, as it can impact the morale of the team and its momentum. The most common reason people to leave a team is that they realize themselves that the agile environment is not for them, and they leave by mutual agreement.

Role of the Product Owner

So if the team is self-organizing what is the role of the product owner? The product owner has overall ownership of the product, the direction it takes, and responsibility for the vision of the product, and the team builds it for him or her.

The product owner is responsible for prioritizing the product backlog, ensuring that the most important user stories are implemented first. The product backlog is an evolving, prioritized queue of business and technical functionality that the team needs to be developed into a system.

The product owner is the sole person who controls the product backlog, while working with the team to understand the changing landscape where it is working.

AGILE PROJECT PHASES AND PHASE GATES

You don't need to be able to see the whole
staircase, just take the first step.
—MARTIN LUTHER KING

Projects following a waterfall lifecycle traditionally have five phases: requirements, design, implementation, testing, and acceptance, with some variations. In an agile project, these phases can happen at any stage of a project.

Agile project phases can be grouped into three distinct phases:

- proof of concept
- explore—adapt—implement
- close

Proof of Concept
The first stage in the proof of concept phase is the visioning meeting. The purpose of the visioning meeting is to create a project charter where a clear vision of the project is put forward, including business-case analysis, risks, assumptions, constraints, costs, and a registry of stakeholders.

The visioning meeting puts forward a vision, and the purpose of the proof of concept stage is to determine whether the reward for realizing this vision outweighs the risks of failure.

This is done by testing many of the assumptions, risks, and constraints in the project charter and validating them to be true or false. For the real risks, it is necessary to determine a course of action to mitigate them in order to increase the chances of success of the project.

Proof of Concept: Minimum Viable Product

A good practice during the proof of concept phase is to create a minimum viable product (MVP), also called a prototype.

This prototype should have the least number of features necessary to validate the assumptions/constraints/risks in the project charter.

Ideally the MVP is demonstrated to customers so that they can confirm whether it will solve the business need outlined in the project charter.

During the process of building the MVP, the project manager can get a better idea of the capabilities of the team. Is it likely the team will work well together? Are more resources needed than initially thought? Are any specialists missing from the team? Does the team need more training for certain technologies?

For projects with high levels of uncertainty, where the team has not worked together before or is working on new technology, the proof-of-concept stage can considerably mitigate risk.

When a project charter is created, there are many unknowns. The proof-of-concept stage helps shed light on these unknowns and provide the necessary information to the project sponsor as to whether the project should get the green light.

The phase gate at the end of the proof-of-concept stage is essentially a decision based on everything that has been learned. Does the reward for completing this project outweigh the risk of failure? If the answer is yes, then the project proceeds to the next phase.

Now that you have your MVP and are confident that you can build all the features of the product, it is time to create a strategic plan for the project.

This happens during the release planning meeting. The release planning meeting is where the strategy for the project is decided. Where will the focus be first? What are the major sections of the project? How long will they last, and what will determine success?

The release planning meeting takes a medium- to long-term view of the project and should involve senior stakeholders. The reason for their involvement at this stage is that the reporting level to senior management is often at the release level.

Each release is defined at a high level and shouldn't need to change for at least the length of a release, after which the release plan can be reviewed.

Releases don't cover the details of implementation but rather the scope of the functionality. For example, in a student administration system, a release could focus on a component that manages enrollment, and another could manage exams or perhaps coursework. Each release may include tens of user stories and cover a number of iterations.

Once the releases are determined, they are added to the project charter that is presented to the project sponsor for sign-off with an updated list of risks, constraints, assumptions, and costs.

After sign-off, the work to create the team and assign resources for the project begins.

Phase: Explore—Adapt—Implement

The explore, adapt, and implement phase is where the team takes center stage.

At this stage, resources will have been assigned to the project, and the team will be awaiting direction.

Iteration zero is where the team determines their ground rules: values, rules, and structures that the team will put in place so that everyone understands what is expected. These include:

- deciding as a group a common set of values,
- gaining a common understanding of the project vision and the goals for the team,
- deciding what agile processes will best suit the team and determining if any training is needed, and
- determining what the meeting commitments are for the team and why they are important.

It is the team that decides the ground rules. The success or failure of agile teams is judged at the team level rather than at the individual level, so it is important to empower the team to self-organize under the guidance of a good coach. If the team decides its values and rules, it is much more likely to follow them. It is the role of the coach to ensure that the team puts enough structure in place to create a greater likelihood of success of the project.

Explore—Adapt—Implement: Release Planning Meeting for Release X

During iteration zero, the team focuses on creating the user stories that it will need to implement in the current release, while also keeping in mind the bigger picture and future releases.

The release planning meeting for release X is led by the product owner. With the help of the team, all the user stories for this release will be defined, sized, and prioritized, with a number of approaches that we will look at later.

The outcome of this meeting is a clearly prioritized list of user stories that can now be implemented by the team.

At the end of iteration zero, the first iteration planning meeting is held. In this meeting, the product owner again reviews the product backlog and determines what the most important user stories are that need to be implemented first. After clarifying any uncertainties in the user stories, the team as a whole makes a commitment as to what they can achieve with the guidance of the coach.

At this point, the team is ready to implement the product owner's highest-priority user stories. This is essentially the phase where the product outlined in the project charter is created following an iterative process of exploration, execution, and retrospection.

At the start of each iteration, the highest-priority stories are scheduled to be implemented. During the iteration, daily stand-ups are held to ensure there are no impediments for the team and that it is making progress. At the end of the iteration, features are demonstrated to the product owner and, finally, the team holds a retrospective to see what it can do better in the next iteration. The team continues in this iterative fashion until this phase is complete.

Close Phase

The close phase in an agile project can vary in duration and content, depending the on the project.

For projects such as hardware projects, a phase of releasing the product to the market needs to be completed as part of closing off the project. During each iteration, releases will have been made to customer representatives on the team or focus groups, but it may not have been possible to release the product until it was finished. If the team was following agile principles to the letter, then components of the project should have been integrated and tested and confirmed as done-done at the end of each iteration, so there should be a need to refocus efforts here.

For other projects, frequent releases to customers means that when project development is nearing the end, 99 percent of the functionality will have been live for some time. Features will have been pushed live from the first iteration and may even be on the second or third version as the product responded to market/customer reaction.

For projects that fall into this category, the close phase involves a few simple steps:

- Close phase: project retrospective
  The project retrospective gives the team a chance to look at lessons learned on the project and document them for future reference. This creates a chance to contribute to the company knowledgebase what approaches where successful and could be implemented again on future projects, and which should be avoided and why.
- Close Phase: Release Staff
  If the team is disbanding to other work, this would have been planned for some time, and the close stage of the project will involve a process of releasing the staff to other teams. However, it is often a good idea to keep teams in place if there are suitable projects to assign to them, as it takes time to create a highly functioning team.
- Close Phase: Tidy Up
  The code and tests need to be checked in, environments decommissioned, working space tidied up, index cards shredded, and hardware and office space reassigned.
- Close Phase: Celebration!
  Providing that the project was a success or at least lessons were learned, when everything is done-done-done, it is time to party! A chapter has closed; mark it with style by recognizing your team with a social event.

VISIBILITY AT A GRANULAR LEVEL: USER-STORY CARD TEMPLATE

A lack of transparency results in distrust
and a deep sense of insecurity.
—DALAI LAMA

S ome people prefer to use software to manage the agile project management process, and others prefer an information wall. Sometimes a combination of the two is essential.

An information wall or information radiator allows the team to share information with anyone who walks in the room. If user stories are written from the product owner's perspective, they should be understandable to anyone with some knowledge of the domain.

Having an open attitude to information and project progress promotes understanding among colleagues and encourages interaction.

Many companies these days outsource some of their development team so a software approach may also be necessary in managing the agile process. Software can also be helpful for automating reports that are sent to senior management.

Structure of the User-Story Card

One of the principles of agile project management is simplicity. For the user-story card, it is a matter of including the least amount of information that conveys enough detail for anyone to understand it.

Some user-story cards hold only the name of the user story, a brief description, and its size. Other teams prefer more detail. Some of the most common information included is below.

The Fields: User Story

User Stories should be ideally written by the product owner with the help of the developer.

A helpful format is:

I, as a (role), want (function) so that (business value).

When the product owner writes the user stories, it means he or she understands it, has more buy-in, and is more likely to be comfortable signing off on it.

The Fields: Planned Iteration and Iteration Dates

Leave plenty of room in these fields to cross out the iteration number or dates should a story not get finished in an iteration. It is important to see the dates, as the numbers alone will mean little to someone outside the team.

The Fields: Story ID and Story Points

If you are using computer software and an information wall, the Story ID should be the same. The story points are the relative size of the user story relative to others. One is the smallest, and higher numbers are multiples of the smaller user stories.

The Fields: Story Details

This should be written by the product owner with the help of the team and should outline any additional details of the user story that are needed to starting building a solution. These are high-level details. The developers will talk to the customers while building the tool to sort out the details.

The Fields: Uncertainty Factor

This is important as it estimates the accuracy of the user-story size. Generally the value is a percentage increase. For example, if the uncertainty factor is one, it means the user-story estimate can vary by 10 percent. If it is zero, it means the team is certain of the size.

The Fields: Dependencies

It is arguable whether or not this should be included, because dependencies should be avoided at all costs. It is preferable to create a larger user story than have one that is dependent on others. The reason is that it is not possible to integrate or release a story that depends on others, nor is it possible to declare it done-done.

The Fields: Relative Value

The relative value is an important field. It defines the relative value to the customer of one user story over another. These are important within epics as they determine the likelihood of a user story being completed as part of an epic. The user stories with the highest-relative values should be at the top of the product-backlog list (priority queue). It is a good idea to make how this number is determined as quantitative as possible.

For example, if you are comparing the relative importance of fifty stories, rather than arbitrarily choosing a relative value, follow this process:

- Decide on how you will compare the relative values of user stories. (i.e., increase income, increase efficiency, better user experience, or more traction).
- Decide the relative weight of these comparators.
- Bring the product team together to assign values to these comparators, and you will end up with a relative value.

This process stimulates debate and generates a better understanding of user stories.

When the process is over, the product owner can change the relative values as he or she has authority over the product backlog.

The Fields: Epics and Releases

Epics and releases are a higher level of abstraction for the product backlog.

Iterations are often between one and four weeks in length. Story epics are multiples of three to five times this, and releases are multiples of three to five times the length of a story epic.

The higher you go, the more abstract the description becomes, and the less likely it is that the description will change.

In the same manner as an iteration, story epics and releases are time-boxed, which allows for better planning. If all the stories for an epic are not completed by the end of the epic, the lower-priority stories may be dropped.

By the nature of agile project management, the most important ones will have been implemented first as part of the process.

Flexibility can be included for epic and release dates if the product owner and sponsor agree with the additional cost. This is unlike an iteration length, which should never be changed.

The Fields: Acceptance Tests

When a user story passes these tests, it is ready for release. It is helpful to make the tests as clear as possible. It is the product owner's decision if a user story has been satisfactorily completed. It is the project manager's responsibility to explain the cost of bringing the user story into the next iteration.

VISUALIZING THE PROJECT WITH THE AGILE PROJECT DATA SHEET

The problem with a project charter as a document is that it is not suitable for pinning to an information wall.

One of the main features of agile project management is that projects are transparent to everyone who is part of the team, a stakeholder, or a passive observer. This transparency builds trust from your colleagues, encourages engagement, and reinforces the team's commitment to its goals.

One way to achieve this transparency is through an information wall, often called an information radiator.

The information wall is where you put your project priority queue; the tasks that are planned for the current iteration; the product backlog; and, generally, anything that is useful to communicate the progress of the team and what is currently being worked on.

Having a project charter as a document is useful as it is the easiest way for one person to read the outline of the project. The agile project data sheet offers an unchanging list of facts about the project: its objective, vision, scope, and direction.

Teams approach the project data sheet in different ways. Below are some of the most common fields for the project data sheet.

Product Vision
The product vision for a project seldom changes. It is the thirty-second elevator pitch of what the product will do once it has been built. It is the pitch that the product owner made to the project sponsor in the first place and what won the funding to start the project. It is a few simple sentences that outline what the product does and why people should care.

Project Objective
The project objective is a clear outline of what the project will have accomplished once it is finished. Whether it is building a product or improving a process, the project needs to have a clear outcome, and that is outlined here.

Business Objective
Completing the project costs money, so the project must contribute to the business's operations in some way in order to be funded. The primary business objectives that this project will reach will be outlined here. Please note that the idea is to put this agile project data sheet somewhere visible, so putting this business objective on the data sheet means you are committing in a public way to deliver it in front of your peers.

Trade-Off Matrix
The trade-off matrix is a simple yet powerful concept that communicates to the team what factors are flexible in a project and what ones are not. Generally, one item should be fixed (i.e., cannot change), one is flex (room for some change), and one is accept (we accept change in this category). This matrix makes it clear to management which of these factors is of the highest priority, and which change will be accepted in.

Perhaps the schedule is the highest priority, and budget is flexible, and scope can change. If a project comes under pressure, perhaps only 80 percent of the user stories in the project backlog will be implemented, and a 10 percent extra cost will be incurred.

Instead, perhaps scope is the highest priority, and schedule is flexible, and cost can change. In this case, all the user stories will be implemented. Costs could vary widely, even by more than 100 percent of the original estimate, depending on how much is known about the domain. The schedule can vary to less that 100 percent.

The project-delay cost per month is an important factor in software projects and is usually easy to quantify. The majority of staff are personnel and often they are dedicated to the team.

Exploration Factor
The exploration factor is an important indicator for the team and for management. This correlates directly to the amount of change for the flexibility and accept elements of the trade-off matrix.

The exploration factor is how much is unknown in a project and how much exploration is necessary to fill in the gaps.

It is important that the team has sign-off on this number as management will want it to be as low as possible. Only the team can truly estimate the exploration factor of a project.

Capability
The capability is the major features the project will complete.

Quality Objectives
Quality is usually a set of unquantifiable guidelines for the team to keep in mind as a guide for quality, such as the app must have a "wow" factor,

transition between pages must be smooth, or presentation must have polish.

Performance Guidelines

Performance guidelines are quantifiable and verifiable. For example, the uptime for a site should be 99 percent or the transition between pages of an app should be less than a quarter of a second.

Major Project Milestones

Individual user stories, their details, and positions on the priority queue may change in a project, but the overarching themes and milestones usually remain consistent for the duration of a project. Outlining these in the agile project data sheet gives an overview of the structure of the project.

Architecture Guideline

Who will we build the project for?

Issues and Risk

What are the factors that could derail the project that everyone needs to be made aware of?

Refactoring, Technical Debt, and Slack

Technical debt is inevitable in all projects, and there is no good debt. Technical debt is where the solution to a problem is created in a less-than–optimal way. It has been created in such a way that might cause the team pain in the future, or it might be passive technical debt and never come up again.

Technical debt is caused by pressure to get things done quickly or inexperience that causes a less-than-ideal technical solution to be implemented.

Sometimes it is done knowingly. In such cases, it may be because of pressure to keep a project to a timeline or pressure to keep a project within budget. In such circumstances, the quickest solution may be adopted rather than the best solution. Perhaps a shortcut is taken on commenting code, or a test for test-driven development is not implemented. Or, more generally, a problem may not be fully thought through due to time pressure, resulting in problems with the code that may resurface down the line.

Technical debt can also be accrued unknowingly due to lack of experience or simply due to the pace of changing technology. A solution may be the best according to the tools and best practice today, but perhaps a better approach will be discovered tomorrow.

When a new person comes on board who is unfamiliar with the workings of the team, that person will likely not meet the standards of the team in all regards from the start. This may lead to problems with the code that needs to be revised in the future. The team will thus incur technical debt.

When a team starts working on a project, the customer likely does not have a complete idea of what the final product will look like and drives the team down a few blind alleys. This can incur technical debt because, as the old saying goes, "If I knew I was going there, I wouldn't start from here."

In software projects, new technology will always incur technical debt. It is impossible to hit it out of the park when you pick up the bat for the first time, and most software projects involve occasionally adopting new technology. If you look back on your code at a future date, you will probably think of better ways to write it.

The management style can also incur technical debt. The style of managing software projects is changing nearly as fast as the technology in this unique field. Are you using test-driven development, agile methods, scrum, kanban, or pair programming? Maybe a new style that gets discovered tomorrow helps developers produce better code faster. In that circumstance, what do we do with the code we already have?

Refactoring

Refactoring is the process of paying off technical debt. It is the process of looking at old code and seeing if it can be done better, more efficiently, or using new methods.

In agile teams, the code belongs to the team, so anyone can refactor anyone else's code. If your team is following a test-driven development approach, it really helps when refactoring. This is because refactoring should not change the output of existing code, but instead the manner in which the output is achieved. It's about the style rather than the substance.

Test-driven development means that the set of tests can be run after the refactoring is complete to ensure that the code still does what it was originally written to do.

At first glance, refactoring may look like a nice idea but something that a busy team may not have time for. So when do we do it?

Slack

Every software team needs to keep slack in its development process. This helps the team stay on a steady velocity and gives management something reliable to plan against. Refactoring code for one hour a day is a good way to manage slack. If the team comes under pressure to maintain its velocity, then refactoring can be dropped for a few days without any impact on the team's output.

Having team members refactor each other's code is a great method for them to learn from each other and improve together.

TECHNICAL DEBT AND PAIR PROGRAMMING

T echnical debt is defined as the eventual consequences of poor system design, software architecture or software development within a code base. There are many reasons for technical debt, which include the following:

- Programmer inexperience. Programmers or teams may incur technical debt as they gain experience and get up to speed with a project.
- Tools may be inadequate. Software tools evolve. A certain amount of technical debt can be incurred due to the limitations of the tools that are chosen and used.
- Lack of resources assigned to a project, be it time, money, processes, infrastructure, or personnel, mean that technical standards needed to be dropped in order to meet requirements.
- Manager inexperience. When a manager has a deficit of experience in managing software projects, this often leads to technical debt because inadequate resources or processes are applied to the project,
- Programmer fatigue. Programmers are often optimists and will promise more than they can deliver. This means they will have to work harder than normal to meet their targets. The output they produce is then expected in future software release iterations, and, over time, they burn themselves out. This leads to technical debt.

Technical debt can never be completely overcome, but there are a number of approaches that you can take to ensure you incur the least amount possible. One such approach is pair programming.

Pair programming is where two people work off one machine. One is the driver, and the second is the navigator. The driver writes the code, and the navigator guides the programming process. A pair may stay together for a day, and they generally switch position of coder and navigator regularly. On the following day, new pairs will be assigned.

When managers hear about pair programming, they think, "Surely it will lead to half the work being done," and when programmers hear it will be introduced, they are concerned about someone looking over their shoulders or that they will be embarrassed by any limitations they have.

Actually the result is often the opposite of both concerns. Productivity increases when pair programming is introduced, and the quality of the work produced increases dramatically. Pair programming ensures that over time, skills and expertise are transferred across the team and the team becomes a superstar performer rather than an individual. Pair programming means the team, rather than the individual, is the real asset of the organization; however, a prerequisite of a performing team is performing team members. Everyone wins.

SPIKES, TASKS, AND BUGS

At the most granular level, the agile approach to project management boils down to answering three simple questions: What will I do today? What did I do yesterday? And what issues came up?

So for the purpose of morale, it is important that tasks are broken up so that everyone has something positive to report during the daily scrum. For this reason, it is usually a good idea to try to break tasks down into work that will likely last one day at most.

So how long is the average ideal day? How many hours of productive work are done on average? On a well-performing team, the best you can hope for is four to six hours of productive work.

This may not always be possible. Some tasks will take longer than a day, and it may not be a good idea to break them up. In these cases, be careful to not have the same people working on the longer tasks all the time.

Iterations involve delivering a shippable product; this means that the bugs must not exceed a certain number and that quality must match the company's policies and standards. Within reason, bugs need to be fixed during the iteration in which they were discovered, especially if they relate to the tasks that are being worked on.

When that's not possible, then a new user story needs to be created, and the bug will be placed on the product backlog. Since only completed stories contribute to the velocity of the team, the team will want to resolve all issues in the current iteration where possible.

When estimating for tasks or for user stories, it is always best to get the people who will actually do the work to make the estimate. Planning and estimating meetings should be team events to get team commitment to the timeline and involve as much knowledge and experience as possible.

An unusual, but often necessary, task a team member needs to do in an iteration is research new technology or a new approach. These are often called spikes.

Section 2
Metrics, Management and Organization

METRICS FOR AGILE TEAM PERFORMANCE

Measure what is measurable and make
measurable what is not so.
—GALILEO

According to conventional measures of cost, time, and functionality of a product produced by a project, very few projects can be judged to be successful.

The problem with using these metrics is that for complex projects, there will be a multitude of variables that will not be known at the beginning of the project when they are set, which makes the probability of success highly unlikely. All they can measure is the degree of failure.

One way of measuring performance in a software project is suggested by Lawrence Putnam. This model is called the SLIM model. It has five characteristics with which to measure success:

- quantity of function: scope measured in terms of user stories that are completed during the project
- productivity: expressed as user stories completed for the time and effort (team velocity)
- reliability: expressed in terms of the defect rate

- time: the duration of the project in calendar months
- effort: the amount of effect expounded in person months

These simple metrics provide a pulse that will measure how any project is performing at any point in time, and they are easy to measure. The first three are mostly within the control of the team and are reasonable measures of progress.

However, if the purpose of the metrics is to give an overview of the current state of the project and to give warning signs that it may be going off track, the metrics are incomplete.

For teams that adopt agile methods, the commitment that management shows to a project is vital to its success. Whether it is resources, a suitable product owner, or attendance at meetings, the necessary commitment from management to a project needs to be outlined at the outset and measured during the course of the project. This metric is called management commitment. If management commitment drops, the other metrics within the team's control are likely to follow.

Another metric that is missing from the list is a measure of value that has been delivered through the project. Over the course of the project, the product owner can assign a relative value to each user story during the release planning stage. This then gives the team the ability to release user stories that provide a measurable degree of value to the customer. The product owner acting on behalf of the customer has complete control over the product backlog and can reprioritize it at any time. Because the product owner is part of the project team, this means that the team has control and responsibility over the outcome of the project and the value it delivers to the customer. This metric is called customer value (outcome). Measuring customer value means there will be no surprises late in a project about the value a project has delivered.

AGILE PROJECT MANAGEMENT REPORTING AND CONTROL

In dwelling, live close to the ground. In thinking,
keep to the simple. In conflict, be fair and generous.
In governing, don't try to control. In work, do what
you enjoy. In family life, be completely present.
—LAO TZU

One benefit of taking an agile approach to a project is that it allows for a great deal of flexibility at the granular level while maintaining a level of consistency and predictability at higher levels.

The main problems a new agile team face is lack of training and lack of senior management buy-in. Unfortunately, lack of training can lead to lack of confidence in agile from senior managers.

What often happens is that project managers consistently manage the daily stand-up meetings and processes around iterations, but these involve a high level of change. Reporting on these activities may make senior managers worry that the project is out of control because they are uncomfortable with the level of change. However, agile project management is predicable at a high level and gives senior management the control they need at every stage.

The agile methodology allows teams to tailor their approaches to their needs. Below is a list of the overarching steps in the process, and following that we will describe the scenarios where each is applicable:

- daily stand-up meetings
- iteration
- wave
- epic
- release
- charter (visioning document, product data sheet)
- portfolio
- program

Daily Stand-Up Meetings

The daily stand-up meetings are attended by all members of the agile team. The purpose of the meetings is for members of the team to share their progress on tasks and what is impeding them in their work. This is done by asking the team the following three questions:

- What did I accomplish yesterday?
- What will I do today?
- What obstacles are impeding my progress?

The daily stand-up is the most granular level meeting in the agile process. On a daily basis, a huge array of problems may occur, and tasks may or may not get done, but by having a daily meeting, problems can be resolved quickly and impediments removed.

Making a daily commitment to your teammates about what you plan to achieve on any given day creates a powerful momentum where everyone is doing their best to keep their commitments.

It also creates an environment where if a teammate is having a problem or issue, a fellow teammate may have the answer to resolve it. Because issues are raised frequently, they are also quickly resolved.

When members of the team share what they are working on, other members may be able to share insights and knowledge about how they solved a similar issue before. In a case where there was no problem to begin with, but the mechanism of a daily stand-up meant that the task was solved in a more substantial way for having shared it with your teammates. This produces the effect of the team being greater than the sum of its parts.

In some agile teams, the story points are at a high enough level of granularity for reporting, and this reporting is made to the project manager (i.e., one user story was completed today). In other projects, the user stories are broken down into tasks, and the completion of these tasks is the reporting mechanism at this level (five tasks where completed today).

The degree of change at the stand-up meeting level is where team members make commitments to complete tasks but fail to complete them or perhaps complete them quicker than anticipated. Sometimes these tasks are completed, other days they are not, and a commitment will be made to complete it the following day.

Iteration

Iteration length can vary from one project to another, but the iteration length for one particular project must remain the same for the duration of the project. There are a number of factors that influence the choice of iteration length:

- Length of the longest user story: This is because there should be a capacity to complete a user story during iteration.
- Availability of stakeholders to attend: Iteration planning and demo meetings require the product owner and other stakeholders to be present. The availability of these people is a factor in iteration length.

The most common iteration length is two weeks. This means that there is enough time for building and testing of features in a ten-day working cycle. The reporting at this level is in user stories that are completed (story points), and the reporting is done to the product owner and project manager.

At the start of each iteration, a planning meeting is held, at which the product owner decides what the highest priority user stories should be implemented next. The element of change at this level of the process is that the most important user stories to implement next may change in the product backlog.

Epics, Waves, and Releases

The wave and epic levels are user stories that are grouped together in common functional groups and time-boxed. In large projects, epics and waves may be required. In smaller projects, only story epics may be required.

Releases are when product is released to real customers. This can happen at the iteration level for software products and sometimes at a much longer interval, for example, in the case of hardware products.

For a project of six-months' duration (or less), it may be possible to just have releases every three iterations. These would mean there would be six releases during a six-month project.

Each release would be a collection of similar user stories that are implemented off a product backlog (prioritized list).

Each release is time-boxed. When the release is finished, all the user stories that are finished are released to the users. It is possible that some may not have been completed, but because they are likely to be of low priority, it is less likely to matter to the product owner or senior managers.

This level of reporting is made to senior managers as it is the level that is the most consistent and is in-line with the product charter they signed off on at the start of the project.

If the project is longer than six months, user stories can be grouped into epics, and epics grouped into releases. In this case, epics would last for three iterations and be time-boxed, and reporting would be the same as what was mentioned previously. Releases would be made every three epics.

For even longer projects, the wave level may also be added for a further level of management and control.

Project Charter

The project charter is the document that gives the green light for a project to begin. The project charter will clearly state the control and management processes of the project and what the project sponsor and stakeholders can expect.

Program

The program level is a grouping of similar projects. These projects will be placed in a priority queue, with the most important implemented first. Having projects managed in a program means it is easier to have oversight for the best use of shared resources and common practices. A program of projects is often managed by an AMO (agile management office).

Portfolio

Portfolio project management is the central management of processes, technology, and methods used across a collection of projects. This is often managed by a AMO (agile management office)

MAXIMIZING THE RETURN ON INVESTMENT IN THE PROJECT

A gile project management gives management the most control over managing what the outcome of the project will be in both the short-term and the long-term, therefore maximizing the return on investment.

At the beginning of any project, it is difficult to decide exactly what all the features you might want in the end product might be. The project could take six months or longer to complete, you may not be familiar with the technology or the customer, and the market may change. A long-term plan at this point must be called out for what it is: a guess at a point in time when the least amount of information is available. The chances of this guess being accurate have long odds and do not guarantee a good return on investment.

The agile approach recognizes that there is a huge amount of uncertainty in developing software projects. It looks to keep all stakeholders in the loop as new information is learned, and as the landscape under which the project is executed changes. This ensures that in the short-term, the product owner has complete control over the priorities of the project and what will be delivered, and, over the long-term, the result will be exactly what was asked for, with no surprises.

At the start of each iteration, the team brings everything new it has learned from the previous iteration, and plans and adapts. Some product features may be dropped, some added, and some reprioritized based on the latest information that is available.

The new product knowledge that is gathered in each iteration helps us learn more about what the product should be. New product knowledge is information about the risks, technology, and team and any other lessons learned.

The opportunity for the product owner to alter the priorities for the project at regular short intervals is a powerful contributor to the ability to maximize the return on investment in the project.

Monitoring Application Life Signs with Test-Driven Development

Two things that are often the bane of software developer's lives are testing and documentation.

Why? Because the developer has spent hours, days, weeks writing this amazing piece of code and has spent so much time looking at the tiniest details that the thought of going through all that again fills a developer with dread—and understandably so.

With agile software development there is a way around it. Actually, documentation should be accurately written at a user level when writing the user stories. This should at least provide a description of what the user asked to happen when the software was designed. As part of this process, there are often a number of tests that are informally designed that, if it passes, the software is said to have met the high-level requirements. These can be included in the set of tests for test-driven development. From a user point of view, if these pass, the software works.

Test-driven development formally includes the testing process in the development cycle at the code level; it actually comes before you write production code. The process goes like this:

1. You have the User Story for the function/procedure/application you are building.
2. You write a test that will fail if the function is not there, and pass if it is.
3. This test will be part of a suite of tests that is either run at build time or periodically (weekly). The tests as a whole will highlight if anything has broken in the system.
4. Then you write the code.
5. Run the tests to ensure it passes.
6. Even after an application has gone live, you can set the tests to run periodically and send a report if one of them fails.

Test-driven development helps developers write useful tests while the problem they are trying to solve is fresh in their minds. It helps them think the problem through. These tests are also alive. They are not run once to ensure that code behaved as anticipated at the time, they run during every build and ensure that at any given point, the functionality behaves as it was originally intended.

The report from test-driven development can be a web-page report that can be checked. The website can be a simple table of tests: (1) what is being tested, (2) the results of the last test, and (3) when it was last run. It would also be reasonably easy to include the original overarching customer story to give context. This gives maintenance developers all the documentation they need when they are looking to change the code in the future, and it is alive (if it still passes), which means it is current and up-to-date.

Another benefit of test-driven development is that it gives a developer who is working on refactoring code the confidence that he or she has not broken the core functionality. The developer can run the tests before making refactoring changes; make the changes; and then be confident that, after making the changes, if all the lights are green, the code has been improved and how it behaves has not changed.

Test-driven development fully integrates documentation and testing into the development cycle and makes these processes purposeful for the developer. It effectively gives live vital signs to management and the development team as to the health of the application. It fundamentally removes the pain of conventional documentation and testing for developers!

Organic Risk Management

The pessimist complains about the wind. The optimist expects it to change. The leader adjusts the sails.
—John Maxwell

Risk management is fundamentally different during an agile project compared to a traditional waterfall-based project, largely because of the impact of the last-responsible-moment principle.

Leaving things to the last responsible moment means that decisions are made at a point in time, whereas making the decision any later would have a negative impact on what is being decided.

The effect of leaving things until the last responsible moment is that the most information is available that will help inform the decision and ensure it is the correct one. The availability of the information mitigates the risk.

In a traditional project, the risk-management process begins at the start of the project when the least amount of information is available. A process to examine all the risks that may impact a project is undertaken, and steps to avoid, mitigate, transfer, or accept this risk are outlined.

In an agile project, risk is managed at an appropriate level of abstraction in each stage of the project. When the project charter is being drawn up, what could impact the project as a whole?

When the release planning meeting is undertaken, what could impact the major milestones that are part of the release plan? At the iteration planning meeting, the risks that impact the user stories that are being implemented are discussed. Finally, at the daily stand-up meeting, the team tells the project manager what is currently standing in its way that is creating a risk that the work will not get completed.

During each stage of the process, the project manager asks, "What assumptions are we making, and what concerns do we have?" These questions are asked at stages of the project where the answers will have a direct impact on the work that is about to be undertaken.

The frustration with traditional documentation in software project management is that it is out of date as soon as the ink dries. What is refreshing with the agile approach is that the questions are being asked at a point when the answers are actionable. The answers matter and will not be put in a drawer where they will gather dust.

There are four generally accepted key areas of risk in project management:

- schedule risk
- personnel risk
- specification risk
- scope creep

Schedule Risk
When you are estimating the schedule at the start of an agile project, the accuracy of the estimate will depend on how long the team has been together and whether they have a known velocity in completing story

points. If it is a new team, the ability to accurately estimate a time frame is made less accurate by the number of variables involved in the estimate.

Three or four iterations into the project will give a clear velocity of the team, and the burn-down chart will emerge and give an idea of the time frame at any one point in time.

Personnel Risk

All projects lose staff at different times during the process. In an agile project, this risk is naturally mitigated by the fact that all roles are shared by the team. If the database specialist is busy, the GUI developer may design a database table. If the Linux specialist is busy, the Java developer may update a Cron job. Ideally the project team shares a workspace, so knowledge is transferred all the time, and, if anyone who is unclear about something can lean over the desk and ask.

The open, frequent, and purposeful meetings that are part of the agile project management process also ensure that all members of the team are aware what fellow teammates are working on and/or having problems with. Everyone is on the same page as everyone else, and this ensures that if someone leaves, others can pick up the slack with relative ease.

The flip side is also true for new people who join the team. The open and transparent nature of an agile team means they will quickly get up to speed with the challenges and work at hand.

Specification Risk

The product owner plays a central role in an agile project. This person decides the order of the product backlog (priority queue) and what will be implemented next. It is best practice for this to be one person rather than a committee so it is easier to have a clear chain of command in the decision-making process and so the meetings can be more easily managed to avoid any risk on the specification for the product.

Scope Creep

The scope in an agile project is documented in the product backlog and at a higher level in the release plan. The product owner has ownership over both of these and decides their priorities. It is the role of the project manager to ensure the product owner is aware of what impact an addition of a feature to the product backlog will have on the cost and time frame of a project. If a user story is moved up the product backlog, which user stories will get implemented later as a result should be clearly visible to the product owner.

The product backlog (priority queue) always has the most important features at the top and the least important at the bottom. So if time runs out for the project or a release, the least important features are dropped, creating the least risk for the product. The risk is low that high-priority features will not be implemented.

Agile project management empowers the team to do its job. The product owner has the authority to decide what the end product will look like and is given the tools to exercise this authority. The project manager's role to ensure the project is completed successfully by ensuring everyone has the information and tools needed to make decisions and do their jobs.

Changing requirements are inevitable on a project. The difference with an agile project is that it accepts this fact and empowers the person who can decide what the scope is to make decisions at the right moments about whether or not they need to be changed.

Empowered Agile Procurement

Procurement for agile and non-agile projects is largely the same, with a few distinct differences that we will go through in this section.

One principle of agile project management is empowering people to do their jobs. This principle applies here too. When the project is acquiring a product or service in the process of completing a project, it is generally a good idea to bring the team into the procurement process.

This is valuable because the team brings a diverse set of skills and expertise to the table that will ensure the buying decision is the most-informed it can be. It also has the effect of distributing the knowledge of the process of procurement and brings a sense of group ownership to the buying decision.

If you are an agile seller who sells custom-made software solutions, you need to be careful in managing the expectations of the customers and introducing them to the agile process. This may be your customers' first exposure to an agile project, and they may be nervous of the unknown.

Customers are often surprised at the level of involvement they are expected to commit to. It is usually a good idea to have a face-to-face meeting early on to explain the process and ensure that both parties are happy to commit to it.

Many companies will include the level of commitment necessary for a project in the contract, and they may also include continue-or-cancel options at the end of each iteration. The buyer may cancel if the agile seller fails to make deliveries, and the seller may cancel if the buyer is not giving the necessary commitment to the process.

Overall during the process, buyers will gain exposure and confidence in the agile methodology as it gives them more control over the products they are purchasing.

When an agile team is purchasing a product or service, it may include a retrospective with the supplier at the end of the contract to learn from the process and to see what could be improved for next time. This may also be stipulated in the contract.

AGILE HUMAN RESOURCES: TURNING GOOD PEOPLE INTO GREAT TEAMS

True Motivation Comes From Achievement, Personal
Development, Job Satisfaction, and Recognition.
—FREDERICK HERZBERG (1923–2000), US PSYCHOLOGIST

Our Values

Working in an agile team is not for everyone, and some people will be truly uncomfortable in that environment. People who thrive on an agile team are self-motivated team players who are willing to learn something new and are happy to work in a fluid and changeable environment.

Agile project management is value-driven as opposed to traditional project management, which is plan-driven. Being value-driven doesn't stop at making delivering value a focus point for every project; it permeates everything to do with the project.

For example, scrum projects (Scrum is a form of Agile) have the following five values that are the basis for its practices: commitment, openness, focus, courage, and respect. When adding someone to a scrum team, it is important to determine if the new hire is aligned with these values.

Extreme programming (another form of Agile) is based on the following five principles: communication, feedback, simplicity, courage, and respect.

Many organizations have values, but what is different with agile teams is that these values are fully integrated into all the processes that the team uses on a daily basis. If you were unaware of these five principles, you would probably come up with similar values yourself after using agile methodologies for a period of time. The real strength of agile is that it has constructive values that permeate all the processes.

Defining the Team's Goals and Values

It is important to empower your team and give them ownership of the process. A good exercise when setting up an agile team is to have team members come up with their own goals and values that they believe in.

This can be done when the team is deciding its ground rules at the start of a project.

The process is as follows: Ask team members to visualize that they are at the Annual Software Team Achievement Awards. Ask them to imagine being there with their team in a room with one thousand other agile project members. Then their team is called up. What award will they be receiving? What achievement would they like to be recognized for? What goals did they reach to win it? Get team members to write their answers down on cards and hand them up at the end of the process. Mix them up, read them out, and discuss the result. This removes embarrassment, shyness, and the person from the process and helps dig out great ideas.

Transitioning from a Type-X Manager to Type-Y

According to Douglas McGregor, a management professor at MIT, in theory, X employees are lazy and will avoid responsibility if they can. This may be true in some cases where doing things associated with the work itself does not achieve the sense of personal fulfillment. In such cases, motivational tools such as money or other bonuses are used to motivate an employee to do more.

Theory Y suggests that people are generally self-motivated and desire to do well, given the opportunity. Members of agile teams are often highly motivated self-starters. They are professional and well-paid. The motivation in their case usually comes from a sense of achievement, personal development, job satisfaction, and recognition. It is the responsibility of the agile project manager to create an environment where these motivators can be identified and encouraged.

Every individual has a different set of things that motivates him or her to move forward as a professional. It is the job of the agile project manager to create an environment where team members can find their own personal motivations and remove obstacles so that they can reach their full potential.

A unique motivator in the professional environment where an agile methodology is adopted is the sense of responsibility to the team. The team makes commitments and the team achieves goals, and it is up to each individual to play his or her role. Anyone who has ever played a team sport knows the satisfaction of digging out a win when fellow teammates are having a bad day, knowing they will return the favor in due course. Celebrating your wins with teammates is much more satisfying than celebrating alone.

The Coach

Picture the coaches in a football game. Before the game, they prepare their teams as best they can to succeed in the game. Their goal is to get the best out of every single team member and to provide an environment for them to achieve their highest performance levels. Sometimes their role is to quietly help players one-to-one, and, at other times to motivate the team as a whole. When his team reaches optimal performance, their job is to remove any obstacles that can prevent them from staying there, and to keep themselves out of the way.

The agile project manager plays the same role for his team. Whether it is removing obstacles in the daily scrum or figuring out better working practices in the iteration retrospective, the end goal is the same—achieve peak performance of the team.

Rewards can be given to the team when they achieve results. This is good and healthy in a working environment where an agile methodology has been adopted.

Helping individuals progress professionally is also good and should not be overlooked. Helping members of the team find their individual goals and motivations and getting them to commit to goals they set themselves in their professional development will help the team and lead to greater job satisfaction.

Office Layout: Room to perform

I n an agile working environment, everything hinges on the performance of the team. Every detail is important. Have a look at your office environment and ask yourself, is it an environment for a well-functioning team?

Traditionally, people dream of having a corner office with some privacy and status. This means you are important and a cut above the rest of the workforce, but, for an agile team, separating any team member from the team can be detrimental to the team's success.

There are many opinions on what makes the best office layout for a team, but the fundamental principle is that it enables easy and open communication.

Cubicles are a big no-no. Unless you are in a sales team and are spending lots of time on the phone every day and need privacy so as not to bother others, then the cubicle walls must come down. When a wall separates employees, it screams, "Do not disturb," and that is the last thing you want if you wish to encourage communication. An open plan is often the best option.

A second thing to avoid is having the desks face the wall or the team's backs facing each other. If you need to turn around and "interrupt" another team member to ask a question, then there is a problem with your office layout. Communication must be the most important thing, and it must be easy and fluid. Create an office layout where people face each other and where they can make easy eye contact and easily hear each other should they wish to talk.

Having an environment where people face each other also means that when a conversation is going on, it is easy for other people to contribute. However someone whose back is turned has to turn around to join the conversation, and this may make him or her feel like an intruder.

Some companies go one step further and remove desk assignment altogether and just have a hot-desk space. This makes it easy for team members to change their seating arrangements and collaborate should they need to. The downside of this approach is that it completely removes individual ownership of a space in the office, which can make team members feel less attached to the workplace and less comfortable.

A middle ground for the hot-desk idea is to have desks on wheels. This gives team members their own private space to put their belongings and manage how they wish, but it also enables team members to reconfigure the office space should they need to.

Overall, whatever office layout you choose, focus on enabling good communication because that is what enables good teams to become great.

An AMO Can Bring Serious Firepower to an Agile Team

A company that is serious about adopting agile project management needs an agile management office (AMO).

Among the primary reasons why an effort to adopt the agile methodology fails in organizations are these two reasons, lack of trained agile practitioners, and a lack of senior management support. For an organization that is looking to support multiple agile teams in their organization, creating an AMO will significantly improve the chances of success and remove these obstacles.

In a project-centered organization having a PMO (project management office) support multiple project teams that provide services like training and support will create efficiencies for project teams. The benefits are amplified even further for agile teams.

An AMO can improve the probability of success of agile teams by doing the following:

- establishing and supporting an agile culture,
- providing a training program to all agile practitioners,
- following developments in the agile industry,
- bridging the gap between senior management and agile teams,
- defining a common reporting standard and ensuring compliance,

- removing anything that blocks or hinders the performance of an agile team, and
- co-ordinating a pool of shared resources.

Establishing and Supporting an Agile Culture

When the agile methodology is first adopted by an organization, it is usually done in a small, controlled fashion with one or two teams. It is important that all stakeholders involved in the trial period have a good understanding of agile practices and what to expect, but it is likely that early-stage trials will not reach everyone in the organization.

When the agile methodology is adopted more widely in an organization, a more controlled and resourced approach to establishing and supporting an agile culture is required, and this is the role of the AMO.

Providing a Training Program to All Agile Practitioners

Many will not have been exposed to the agile manifesto and the agile principles. Training will play a large part in a company-wide rollout of agile practices.

Different organizations may choose to adopt different agile practices, but within an organization, it is important that the approach is consistent. It is the role of the AMO to choose what agile practices are most suitable and to ensure these practices are applied uniformly.

Training is an ongoing effort as the requirements of the organization change and as agile practices evolve.

Following Developments in the Agile Industry

Agile project management is still a relatively new industry, and the majority of companies have used agile methods have done so for less than ten years.

Experts in the industry regularly refine their approaches and find new ways to implement the agile methodology in their organizations. The AMO needs to stay abreast of changes in the industry so the organization can adopt suitable emerging trends to its benefit. The AMO will also ensure that any new practices are introduced consistently across the organization.

Bridging the Gap between Senior Management and Agile Teams

Senior management support is critical to the success of agile teams. Senior management will be familiar with a traditional form of high-level reporting, and this will change when agile practices are adopted.

It is the role of the AMO to provide suitable training to senior managers to ensure they have the information they need to fulfill their roles in a format they can understand and use.

Defining a common reporting standard and ensuring compliance

In an agile project, progress is measured in terms of value, quality, and constraints. It is the role of the AMO to ensure that, as much as possible, reporting is completed in a uniform fashion across teams so that progress can be gauged more broadly across the organization. Inconsistent reporting will create data that is less reliable for senior management.

Removing Anything That Hinders the Performance of an Agile Team

By the very nature of an agile organization, there will be a consistent stream of feedback from stand-up meetings to retrospectives that will tell the organization what is working and what needs to change. Resolving common problems and seizing common opportunities is the role of the

AMO. A functioning AMO will enable the organization to become more agile and adaptable to a changing landscape of opportunity.

Co-Ordinating a Pool of Shared Resources
Finally, similar to a traditional project management office, the AMO is responsible for coordinating the efficient use of specialized resources across an agile team. In most agile teams, the staff is dedicated and can switch roles as the project demands, but, for some unique roles, a level of specialization is required. Database administrators often fall into this category.

AGILE MANAGEMENT, COACHING, AND RESPONSIBILITY

A coach is someone who can give correction
without causing resentment.
—JOHN WOODEN

Although agile approaches to managing projects are more fluid than more-established approaches, there is a well-defined structure. This structure amplifies the strengths of individuals and produces highly functional teams when implemented correctly. However, the approaches to management, coaching, and leadership are fundamentally different for agile teams.

Management

The role most closely related to a traditional project-manager role in most agile methodologies is the role of the product owner. Rather than manage people, however, product owners manage the development of the product. They decide what major themes should be in each release. They decide what features are in each theme and what the priorities are of those themes. They own the product and are responsible for ensuring it is developed correctly, according to their specifications. Using agile approaches, they have complete control of the product, and they have a large role to play in the success of the product.

This is the role most suited for managing reporting to senior management. What is the velocity of the team? Is the project burn-down chart showing that the project is on track? What things are blocking the team's progress? Who in the organization does the product owner need to speak with to ensure the team has everything it needs to build the product that the product owner is responsible for? What features will get cut from the current release?

Using agile methods, the product owner has complete control over the shape of the product but also has complete responsibility and accountability for the resources that are used and the end result. The product owner answers to senior management on the success of the product.

The agile team effectively works for the product owner as the main customer, and it is up to the product owner to use the resources of the team well and efficiently.

Although the product owner manages the team as a unit, he or she doesn't manage the team members individually or the tasks they do on a daily basis. The team is self-organizing and doesn't need that level of management.

Coaching

Using agile methods, the lowest level of management is the team. The team builds user stories that are written and prioritized by the product owner. The team makes commitments in every iteration and release as to what it can produce and is judged as a unit on whether or not these commitments were met. Incentives on reaching commitments should always be awarded to the team as a whole rather than to individuals, thus strengthening and reinforcing the team unit.

The team doesn't need to be managed in the traditional sense, but it does need to be coached to peak performance. This role is often defined as the scrum master.

The coach has a number of key responsibilities, which will be discussed below.

1. Educating the Team on the Agile Method Being Used

It is vital that the team understands the importance of all the characteristics of the agile method being used. Why are the daily stand-ups important? How long should the iteration length be? How frequently should retrospectives be held? It is the role of the coach to ensure the team has full buy-in and accepts the importance of every aspect of the method it is using.

2. Focusing the Team on the Highest Priorities of the Product Owner

The coach has a coaching role for the team. Although the team is self-organizing, the coach needs to keep an eye on the big picture. The coach ensures the team is consistently moving forward in the right direction and that everyone is on the same page as to what that direction is.

3. Running Meetings Effectively and Efficiently in Service of the Team

There are a number of structured meetings that are part of the agile process. Daily stand-ups, demo meetings, retrospectives, release planning meetings, and so on. All these meetings have a defined structure that needs to be managed carefully to ensure they are in the best interests of the team. This is the role of the coach.

4. Removing Barriers that Hinder the Team

During the daily stand-up meetings, the coach will hear what obstacles are standing in the way of the agile team completing its tasks. It is the responsibility of the coach to show leadership and do everything to remove these obstacles. The coach can then report back to the team the

GERALD O'CONNOR

progress on removing these problems and what the status of them currently is. The person who should escalate problems outside of the project team is the product owner. The reason is that the product owner has ownership of the success of the project as a whole. He or she has a personal stake in whether the project is successful. If the coach cannot resolve the issue alone, then he or she needs to raise it with the product owner. If the product owner fails to resolve it, and it hinders the success of the project, then the product owner will be held accountable.

It is important that this chain of responsibility is made clear at the start of the project. The product owner is responsible for the product; the coach is responsible for the team.

5. Introducing Engineering Practices and Adherence (Test-Driven Development, Continuous Integration, Done-Done Code)

The coach is responsible for the performance of the team and the quality of the product it creates. He or she is responsible for introducing technical or nontechnical practices that increase the performance of the team and the quality of the product it produces. The coach is responsible for being aware of practices that may help the team, educating the team on the process, getting buy-in, and rolling out the process successfully.

6. Coaching the Team to Peak Performance

The coach must have all the soft skills necessary to coach the team to peak performance.

This includes the ability to manage all the different personality types and their strengths and weaknesses and ensuring that everyone on the team has a voice and feels like they belong.

Resolving small conflicts, such as a domineering personality in team meetings, and resolving larger personality conflicts are the responsibility of the coach.

102

It is the role of the coach to decide if someone is not the best fit for the team and to ask that person to move on and also to determine if the team is missing a certain type of team member who needs to be added.

The coach can be a member of the team and really should sit with the team. The team and the coach must feel they are part of a unit in order for the team to reach peak performance.

The coach never reports on the team, whether tasks or user stories. These measurements need to be organic (self-organized). If the coach is seen as managing or policing the output of the team, other team members will not view the coach as part of the team, thus putting barriers in place. It is the role of the product owner to ensure that the project is on track and going in the right direction, and it is the role of the coach to ensure the team has optimal performance.

TEAM VALUES: THE FOUNDATION FOR HIGH-PERFORMING TEAMS

Individual commitment to a group effort—that is what makes a team work, a company work, a society work, a civilization work.
—VINCE LOMBARDI

Have you ever been in an office where staff members are complaining about their manager behind his or her back? Or in an office when one individual is labeled the weakest member of the team by his or her colleagues? This can lead to a toxic environment in the workplace and seriously hinder the productivity of your team.

In all work environments, certain negative behaviors can appear when the pressure is on. In an ideal world, how would the team like to be treated in these situations?

One practice that helps remove these negativity tendencies is to help your team agree on a common set of values in the workplace. These are principles with which they would define their ideal place to work.

There are a number of ways to determine team values. Here is one approach:

1. Ask the team members, one by one, to discuss, the best and worst places they have ever worked, and why. Encourage the team to talk about specific scenarios.
2. Then put team members in pairs and ask them to list ten statements starting with, "I don't like it when."
3. Discuss the results, and determine the most common answers.
4. Then assign new pairs, and ask each pair to list ten statements starting with, "I like it when."
5. Discuss the results, and, from these results start to determine a common set of values.
6. It may be necessary for the team lead to take the statements away to condense them into a common set of values that can be discussed in a follow-up meeting.

Examples of team values may include statements like the following:

- We always act as a team and are judged as a team.
- We accept that we don't know everything and are constantly learning.
- We offer constructive criticism one-on-one rather than in a group.
- We help each other reach peak performance.

Once the team has established its values, display them prominently in the workplace where they can act as a regular reminder to team members of what they expect of each other.

The purpose of having team values is to create a work environment that is healthy and positive for every member of the team, creates an environment that helps individuals maximize their strengths, and helps the team achieve peak performance.

SECTION 3
LEARN, MASTER, AND TRANSCEND

SHU-HA-RI

Those who are possessed by nothing possess everything.
—MORIHEI UESHIBA

Nearly every company I've come across that has adopted agile methodologies has applied them in different ways—often in completely different ways, and sometimes missing fundamental components that are common across all methodologies.

Generally, if there is a consistency across companies about an approach to something, in this case that companies take a consistently different approach to agile project management, then there must be merit in doing so—and there is. However, how can a company director or senior manager ensure that the approach that is being adopted will deliver the best results for the company?

In Alistair Cockburn's book, *Agile Software Development: The Cooperative Game*, he makes an interesting comparison between Aikido and agile project management that can help senior managers solve this conundrum.

"Shu"
The term "shu" means learn. This comes first in the process of adopting a practice. During this stage of adopting a practice, the focus is on

mastering the basics of a discipline and coming to a deep understanding of why certain things are done. Whether students are learning XP, scrum or kaban, the first stage is to master the practice, become skilled at applying it, and create a deep understanding of why things are done the way they are.

In agile terms, during this stage, you may be working toward one of the many qualifications in agile methods and aiming to become certified at a professional level of competency.

"Ha"

The term "ha," again from the Akido phrase "Shu-Ha-Ri," means to detach. This follows the mastery phase. During this part of the students' development, the form (i.e., the regimented structure) becomes less important and what enables the best result becomes the highest priority.

At this point, the student understands why a certain thing is done and can make an informed decision about why a certain step in the process may be unnecessary.

For an agile practitioner, changing an established process and methodology without a deep understanding of the process is a recipe for disaster. Changes can sometimes come due to resistance to certain practices or due to a poor understanding of them by management and an inability to convince others that although certain things take effort, they will deliver results. In order to have enough understanding of an established practice that is being followed by a large community, you must have a high level of mastery to ensure that what you leave out will not be detrimental to the process.

"Ri"

The "Ri" portion of "Shu-Ha-Ri" means to transcend. Transcending a practice means going beyond what was originally taught, somehow adding something new that, therefore, creates something different.

In an academic environment, a scholar will try to transcend a field of expertise and publish something new and novel to move the field of expertise forward and to be awarded his or her doctorate. Doing this involves mastering many related fields, generating a deep and thorough understanding, and offering a unique and unprecedented solution to a problem.

For agile project management, transcendence requires mastery of many methodologies to understand how each can be applied to the broad spectrum of problems faced by project managers. After such mastery, the project manager will perhaps have a question that currently isn't answered by the agile body of knowledge, and he or she must transcend it and contribute to it in order to solve the problem.

AGILE TEAM ENERGY AND GAME THEORY

The greatest teams find a way to win.
—ALLAN RAY

Most jobs are about earning a paycheck to pay the bills. You clock in, put in a shift, go home, and have fun on the weekend. If these jobs didn't pay, nobody would do them. Software development is different.

In some professions, more is gained from going to work every day than just drawing a paycheck. Take a professional sports person for example. Yes, it must be amazing to walk out in front of one hundred thousand fans in a Super Bowl final but if these guys didn't have that level of success, they would just as happily walk out on an Astroturf pitch on a wet Tuesday autumn evening for a scrimmage with their friends. It's not money that drives them.

In software development, there are a number of parallels with sport. If there were no financial incentive to develop software, there would still be a thriving community of developers doing so. Take open-source software as an example. In this case, the bulk of the work is done by unpaid contributors who put in long hours for zero financial reward. Another example is the many technical sites where people ask questions, and a thriving community of people rushes to provide answers and improve their status within the community.

Whether at the amateur level of sport or software development, even when the talent on display is threadbare, there is a passionate drive to be better, to compete, and to win. The question is, how do we create such a working dynamic on our professional software teams? How do we tap into this latent energy?

Answering this question is not about figuring out some approach to get more output from your team (that's a side effect), but, instead, it is about creating a work environment that people would turn up to even if they were not paid.

As an example, let's take an agile team of eight people who are tasked with developing a customer relationship management system (CRM) for their company. What are the rules of the game? Here are some:

- the goal: create working software that satisfies the sponsor's needs
- length of the game: a period of time that is agreed to by the sponsor or less (for bonus points),
- keeping score and the competitive element will be discussed next

Competitive Element in Software Development

The most fundamental human desire is to be seen as being good at something, to feel that you have a purpose and that you add value. Whether it is in your family, your pastimes, or in your job, everyone needs to satisfy this need.

Some folks dislike being competitive. They ask, "Why can't we all just get along?" Competition is not necessarily about competing against others. It can also be a drive for self-improvement (i.e., competing against yourself or striving to improve yourself).

Individual Sports

Climbing, for example is sometimes a team sport, but it also can be an individual sport. In the case of an individual, the climber strives to overcome bigger challenges with each climb. The factors that make the climb challenging are mainly nature and the elements. An individual climber is similar to a person who develops code alone.

Team Sport

Coding in a team is similar to a team of climbers, where each member of the team relies on teammates to reach the summit and achieve the group goal. In a team of climbers, there is no individual who wins or loses; instead success—or not—comes to the team as a whole. The sense of achievement when the goal is reached is a shared experience with your teammates; you couldn't have done it without them.

In such an environment, there is a joint sense of ownership. When the team reaches a crisis point, it's not an individual's problem but a team problem, and the members must pull together to resolve it and move forward to achieve their goal.

When you relate this type of team sport to software development, it raises a tricky management problem. How do you give your team new projects that will continually challenge them and that will instill a sense of achievement when a project is completed? Could you imagine a team of climbers climbing the same slope over and over? Wouldn't they get bored? This creates a challenging management problem. Failure to solve it means the team will lose its latent energy.

The result of this failure is twofold. One is that the star players (ambitious employees) will start to feel that they are capable of more than the position offers (and may leave), and second is that less-ambitious players will lose the environment that would have pushed them to be better employees (and may stay), both with negative consequences.

There are a few solutions to this problem. One is to sit down with your team members, one on one, at the end of a project, listening to how they see themselves developing, and setting ambitious goals for them in-line with their personal goals; technically speaking, this is a one-on-one retrospective. Second, look for more-challenging projects for high-performing teams.

There is a third option...

Competitive League Environment

If you work in an environment where there are multiple software-development teams, there is a third option to creating the drive to succeed that often appears in amateur sport. Create a league or a ladder.

Considering the fact that projects will start at different times, a ladder may be the best approach for software teams.

The way it works is that the highest-ranking team is at the top of the ladder, and the worst-performing is on the bottom. In a sports context, it is important to note that there is no financial reward for being at the top of the ladder. Every tennis club has a ladder, and players strive to do better, but it also reflects the reality of the game.

In this type of environment, what would the rules for the teams be to measure performance? Here are a few ideas.

Customer-Satisfaction Rating

For each completed user story, the customer must sign-off on it before it is marked as done. Add a satisfaction rating to this process. (For example, if the user story is marked higher than seven, then it can be marked as completed. Lower than seven, and it goes back into the product backlog.) Average out these ratings to get a score. It is in the customers' interests to mark user stories with a satisfaction-rating higher than seven if they want to see the feature going live.

Commitment-Achievement Rating

At the start of each iteration, the team commits to competing with a certain number of user stories. Meeting your commitments gives you a score of one hundred (100 percent). Less than what you committed to gives you a score out of one hundred, and more means you still reached 100 percent on your commitments.

To avoid the same teams always performing well and others poorly, move employees around after a project is completed. Preferably move the star performer from a top-performing team to a poorly performing one. He or she will likely help raise the standard.

These are just some ideas. Creating such a work environment should make for an interesting work environment and for interesting talk around the water cooler. It could potentially make people come to work early and leave late because they enjoy it.

LEADERSHIP IS ASSUMED, NOT ASSIGNED

A leader is best when people barely know he exists, when his work is done, his aim fulfilled, they will say: we did it ourselves.
—LAO TZU

An agile project manager role is to facilitate and direct a team to achieve a common vision. The vision is created in the project charter at the start of the project and outlines a vision of what the product will look like after the team successfully builds it.

It is the agile project manager's role to ensure that the team has everything it needs to best fulfill its role on the team and complete the tasks at hand.

It is also his or her role to remove anything that may get in the team's way of realizing the vision for the project.

The best term to describe an agile project manager is a coach. It is his or her responsibility to get the best out every team member and to ensure the team as a whole is pointed in the right direction and to redirect it when it gets off track.

The project manager is not necessarily the leader of the team. Agile projects do need strong leadership to succeed. Without strong leadership, the team would be rudderless.

Leaders may emerge at different stages of a project, and this should be encouraged. Perhaps in an iteration that is focused heavily on design, a member of the team with strong capabilities in this area will assume a leadership role that helps the team to make the best decisions at this point in the project. For a user story that has a strong database-design component, a member of the team with strength in this area may take a lead. The role of the project manager during the process is to ensure the team is focused on the priorities set by the product owner and that nothing is hindering productivity.

In an agile team, similar to on any project team, it is important to have a balance of experience. It will bring better results for an experienced developer to be decisive at a crucial point than to leave a void that is filled by a less-experienced developer.

Great Teams

A collection of great individuals doesn't automatically make a great team. A great team is coached to peak performance by a skilled Project Manager, and a team firing on all cylinders is much greater than the sum of its parts.

Great teams are built on trust, ability, and empowerment, with the least important of these factors being ability because a good environment can be an incubator of ability.

Trust is the single most important factor for a functioning team. Trust in each other, trust in the project manager, and trust in the organization. After trust is built, empowerment allows the team itself to complete the commitments it said it would complete, and the project manager gets out of the way.

When a team is in the formation stages, the strengths and weaknesses of team members will be exposed, and this creates a vulnerability that suffocates the natural abilities of the team. As the team members learn of each other's talents and gaps, they gain an understanding of and a trust in each other that will allow each individual's strengths to shine through, and each team member will learn to compensate for a weakness in a teammate.

Agile teams need to place a great deal of trust in each other, because when they commit to certain iteration goals, it is the team as a whole that will be judged as having met its targets or missed them. Perhaps during an iteration someone is unwell, and others need to pick up the slack; perhaps the iteration focuses on user stories that are out of the scope of a team member's skill set, and others need to pick up the slack. Creating an environment where everyone pulls together in a complex environment to achieve a common goal is the role of the coach.

Self-Organizing Teams

The term self-organizing is often misinterpreted in an agile context. Some assume that a self-organizing team is without structure and that anarchy will reign on any project that adopts this approach.

The best way to understand a self-organizing team is a sports context. Take soccer, for example. The coach selects the team, analyzes the opposition, prepares tactics for the team, and trains it before a game.

The coach ensures the team has everything it needs to be at peak performance and that nothing is able to interfere with it. But when the team sets foot on the pitch, it is on its own. The coach can't help now. As Helmuth Graf Von Moltke's famous quote goes, "No plan survives contact with the enemy."

As the game unfolds, different leaders may appear on the pitch. In different contexts, a player may play the role of attacker, defender, or midfielder. At the end of the match, one team will win and one will lose, and the whole team will share the spoils equally. Creating this type of team ethic in development teams is not easy but will bring the greatest results.

If you tried to manage a sports team with a traditional project-management approach, it would involve guessing every move of the opposing team and planning your team's response, and everything would need to unfold as anticipated. Such a plan would be out-of-date as soon as it had been conceived.

THE SUPERHERO SYNDROME AND THE SYSTEMS THINKER

Having strong willpower—having a single-minded determination to see a goal through, to reach a peak, or to achieve anything—is always an asset. It is admirable, and anyone who has achieved anything of substance definitely has it in abundance. However there are limitations to what it can achieve and negative side effects.

Those with strong willpower sometimes also develop the super-hero syndrome. This means that when they come across a problem, they use the power of their will to overcome it. They use a blinkered determination to overcome and conquer the problem. However, because they are solely focused on achieving one thing, they often miss others.

They often fail to solve the problem fundamentally. They get a sense of euphoria when they solve it and are often waiting for the next problem to arise so that they can attack it with the same vigor and get the same sense of euphoria.

In business, for a systems thinker, the system here is the superhero syndrome. The system is one of constantly digging the deep reserves of will and determination to solve a problem. The well never runs dry, because this person is built to thrive on the challenge.

The superhero syndrome is necessary to achieve superhuman feats. Did you know that 90 percent of businesses fail in the first ten years? Overcoming these odds requires a single-minded, determined focus to only accept success as an option.

However, the systems thinker looks at things from a sustainable point of view. Rather than running your car in the red of the rev-counter and risking burning out the engine, the systems thinker looks to run it safely in the green.

When problems come up for systems thinkers, they look at solving them fundamentally so that they never arise again. The systems thinker is most content when there is balance and equilibrium. Using the car analogy, when the systems thinker solves a problem fundamentally, it is like the power of the car has increased, and the output of the system has increased so that although the engine is still running in the green, it is achieving a higher power output.

In the software industry, there is never balance and equilibrium. The industry is fast-paced and is in a constant state of change. New technology appears every day, new markets emerge and collapse, and best practice evolves and changes with the seasons. This environment needs superheroes, those who look at the next problem with the same enthusiasm as they conquered the last. But they also need the systems thinker, who builds a solid foundation for future progress by solving problems fundamentally so that the next challenge is faced on a solid and steady foundation.

Agile project management is a great tool for the systems thinker in the software industry. It offers tools and techniques that continually reflect on the current system, looking to make it better. It builds into the process an acceptance that new problems will arise on a weekly basis and that constant change is the new balance and equilibrium. It manages to keep the rev count of the team at the highest mark of the green while constantly under the pressure of continual change.

The superhero is necessary to chart new, unexplored land, and the systems thinker is necessary to build the foundations from which new heights can be reached.

Generative versus Reactive Learning

In the last twenty years, technology has disrupted many industries. Some industries had been a certain way for many years, and, overnight, everything changed.

It is not just nontechnical companies that are disrupted by a fast-moving tech company. Even industry-leading tech companies that appeared to have had an unassailable position in the market have been disrupted by a competitor who wasn't happy to just react to what was already there, who imagined what had never been and sought to build it.

Take Microsoft office as an example. A few years ago, everyone in business needed a copy of Microsoft Office to create their documents, spreadsheets and presentations. The model was that you paid hundreds of dollars for a license, and then you could use the software with no additional charge from that point on.

Ten years ago, however, cloud-based solutions started to appear that could read and edit Microsoft Office documents. Many were free, but the ones that weren't charged a small recurring monthly fee that included updates and new features. You no longer needed to get all your office applications from one vendor; you could pick and choose what you wanted. The barrier for entry dropped for new competitive offerings, and a richness of choice opened up in the industry. In the end,

Microsoft had to fundamentally change its pricing structure and distribution model to match the new disrupted landscape.

Reactive versus Generative Learning

The software industry changes at such a rapid pace that learning is a part of the job. A new technology appears, and you have to spend a few days learning how to use it in order to keep up with the changes in industry. Most companies accept that staff need to occasionally learn on the job in order to get things done.

However, few companies would accept it if an employee started learning a new technology or approach that wasn't immediately needed. Everyone is busy, and we have deadlines and commitments. *How could the staff member be so self-indulgent?* the manager might think. However, reactive learning means that you will always be behind the curve and playing catch-up.

With many industries undergoing some degree of change, it's necessary for companies to take a broader outlook. Time needs to be allotted for staff to try out new emerging technologies and see how the company can take advantage. In some cases, nothing may come of it; in others, a new opportunity might emerge for the company to take a leadership role.

Feedback Loop

For generative learning to have an amplified affect, create a rule in your company that if anyone who signs up for a few hours of generative learning a week is obligated to do a presentation to the rest of the team once a month, so that everyone can learn from the experience and move forward as a whole. This will not only help the team learn a new skill, it will also develop leadership and presentation skills in the individual and helps to build a stronger team.

When a Project Is Considered a Failure

*I have not failed. I've just found ten
thousand ways that won't work.*
—Thomas A. Edison

So the project you have been working on for the past six months has been canned. You discovered that a core aspect could not be delivered in a commercially viable way. Complete failure...No, not really.

Every project is a brand-new undertaking with a huge amount of uncertainty. The initial preparation for the project is involved in minimizing the risk and increasing the chances of success. It is about increasing the chance of success, but it is impossible to guarantee success 100 percent. Some projects will not deliver on their objectives, but that is all part of project management.

So does that mean they were a complete waste of time? Not exactly. If a project uncovered that there was a fundamental flaw in a business strategy that the company was going to invest in, the short-term failure will result in long-term savings.

A project may have consumed resources in learning that the aim of the project was not possible. This learning is valuable in itself.

The majority of software-development projects involve new technology and are solving completely unfamiliar problems. They involve tons of learning and growing on the part of the team, and this is especially valuable if the team will continue working on projects into the future.

If nothing was learned on the project, then it can be defined as a failure.

A definition of failure for a project from Mike Cohn goes, "A project on which no one came up with any better ideas that was on the initial list of requirements."

SECTION 4
WHY AGILE?

Empower Your Team with Agile Project Management

The growth in agile project management has coincided with a shift in the workforce where knowledge workers (people whose jobs involve handling or using information) have moved toward the empowerment of the workforce, so much so that they can nearly be thought of as volunteers. You need their buy-in to get things done.

Generally, volunteers are thought of as people who do something for the joy of doing it and often don't get paid or need pay for the privilege of doing so. By the nature of the word, volunteers can leave whenever they please. For a knowledge worker, this means leaving and taking the means of production with them—their knowledge. It must be impossible to run a project on such a basis, right? So how does the agile approach to project management instill this altruistic instinct in the people who use it?

Empowerment

Traditional management involves issuing commands to staff to complete tasks, which they do in order to take home their salaries. The motivation is to get paid and provide for their families. The problem is that there is no incentive to work after they have met the basic requirements of their job obligations.

After their basic needs are met, people's most fundamental desires are to be good at something and to look good among their peers. This gives a sense of self-worth. In agile project management, the team is self-organizing. Rather than management telling it what to accomplish every day, the team commits to what it, as a whole, thinks it can complete during an iteration, and everyone works together to meet these commitments.

The actual priority list of work is decided by the customers (project sponsor), because they are the ones who will use the finished product and are paying for it, but the team is empowered to decide what it can actually achieve during an iteration.

In most agile methodologies, the team unit is the lowest level that is managed. The team commits to completing a certain amount of work during the iteration and is held accountable for that. The team should be judged by its successes and shortcomings, not as individuals. If a team member is having a slow week, others need to pick up the slack to compensate. The following week, the roles might be switched. Teams are empowered to do the work, and it is the job of the agile project manager (or scrum master) to ensure that nothing blocks their productivity. If something does, the project manager needs to remove it.

This empowering approach enables individuals to reach their full capacities and enables the team to be greater than the sum of its parts.

Not everyone is comfortable with the agile approach. It only works for motivated individuals who are happy with a high level of transparency in their work. For these individuals, it will give them a real chance to shine. Self-motivated people often see improvements in productivity when an agile approach is adopted, and this energy invigorates the team.

Ownership
During an agile project, the customer (project sponsor) and the team share joint ownership of the direction of the project. With the expert input of the team, the customer decides what the vision of the product

will be and a product backlog of the highest priority features to implement. The team tells the customer how many features it can implement over the next iteration and makes a commitment to do so. The team has ownership of the number of features it can commit to and complete ownership of how these are implemented technically.

Volunteers

Using an agile methodology empowers the stakeholders in the project to have the tools at their disposal to meet their objectives. Everyone is motivated to contribute to the process and attend meetings because they can see how it benefits them. For example, the team turns up to the daily stand-up meetings because they may want the scrum master to remove certain things from their path. The product owner turns up to the iteration planning meeting to ensure that the highest priority features are developed next. The product owner turns up to the demo meeting to check that the features developed in the last iteration meet requirements, and the team turn up to the iteration retrospective to learn from a professional point of view how it can improve and learn from the previous iteration. For a motivated individual, there is value in every part of the process.

The Principles of Agile Project Management

At one point in the software industry, it was thought that the people who made software could be reduced to cogs in a wheel and that a formula could be made to create great software. This has proved incorrect. The focus is less on the product or software and more on the people who make it, the people who want it, and the people who will use it.

The principles of agile project management and planning, as outlined by Mike Cohn in his book *Agile Estimating* are

- individuals and interactions over processes and tools,
- working software over comprehensive documentation,
- customer collaboration over contract negotiation, and
- responding to change over following a plan.

Valuing individuals and interactions over processes and tools highlights the fact that the core of an agile methodology is the people. It is impossible to boil a complex software-development process down to a few processes that can be followed every time and deliver the same results. The main difference in every project will be who is involved and what they bring to the table. That will largely define how the project performs and what it produces.

Working software over comprehensive documentation highlights the complexity of modern software and the fact that it is subject to constant change and progressive elaboration. If the engineers invest lots of time at the start of a project designing the perfect architecture before writing a line of code, you can be sure that as soon as they start to write the code, it will be out of date, and, when they get to the details, the code will be different from the plans, making the documentation irrelevant and misleading.

Customer collaboration over contract negotiation highlights that communication is the core of the agile approach. Regularly discussing new lessons learned and new information means that any contracts that were established at the beginning of a project will quickly become obsolete. This is not just from the perspective of the project team, but also of the product owner. The product owner may learn new market information that may fundamentally change the direction of the product. The agile approach recognizes this, and that is why customer collaboration is a core pillar of the methodology.

Responding to change over following a plan is important because plans are out of date as soon as the ink dries. Field Marshal Helmuth Graf Von Moltke said, "No plan survives contact with the enemy." Why does no plan survive contact with the enemy? Because once you are on the field, the situation is always different. The agile approach emphasizes planning over the plan. In the agile/scrum methodology, the plan changes on a daily basis, and the ink never has time to dry.

YOU CAN'T "PLAN AWAY" UNCERTAINTY

T he joke goes that many software developers wear thick glasses due to poor eyesight, but the joke can be extended to IT project managers who struggle to plan effectively into the future. It just isn't possible to see that far ahead when so many things can change.

Plan—Do—Adapt

Managing a software project needs a fresh approach. If management wants a detailed plan on a large project, it is, of course possible to create one, but make sure to include all the risks and the probability that the project will be over budget +/- 100 percent. Then explain that a better way to manage the ongoing project and to maintain control is to manage what we understand today well, to set goals we know we can reach, and then to bring the new things we have learned into the mix for the next step.

Field Marshal Helmuth Graf Von Moltke sounded like an interesting guy. I would have liked to have met him. Two quotes attributed to him highlight the benefits of the agile approach; first, "No plan survives contact with the enemy." Why not? Because you can never guess exactly what will happen into the medium- and long-term future. The plan can act as a guide, but that's it. Second, and more importantly, "Planning is everything. Plans are nothing." This gets to the core of being agile. Once the plan is a living thing, it is always relevant, it is always accurate, and it is useful. The daily scrum meetings and short sprints ensure that every time you meet the enemy, you have a new plan to defeat them. Charge!

Conventional project-management techniques are well established and have been built around mature industries. The core aspects of construction, for example, change gradually, and much can be learned by previous projects. One can create a plan that spans a number of years, and the plan can lead to completion of a successful project.

Software development, on the other hand, is a rapidly evolving and unique project-management industry. Unlike in other landscapes, it is difficult to see into the distant future and to plan accordingly. The reason is that from one year to the next, so many things change as technology advances.

PLANNING FOR CHANGE

But we made a plan; what do you mean
you can't meet the deadline?
Have you ever heard that in your
work as a project manager?

A "great" project manager in this scenario is one who moves hell and high water to reach the targets, or one who pads the plan with room for the unexpected.

The problem with the first solution is burnout. Inevitably, the stresses of managing an impossible situation will catch up to the individual. Managing the uncertainty by burning the candle at both ends always catches up with you.

Employing the second solution will let things run smoothly. Deadlines will be met, and budgets will not be exceeded. But the problem with padding a timeline or budget is that when you finish early (50 percent of the time), you will nearly always wait for the deadline before handing over the deliverable. This is not just human nature but is also the easiest solution from the product owner's point of view, who will find the project more stable and less work if predicted deadlines appear to be met. The disadvantage is that you will end up spending more resources than necessary. Inevitably the padded initial estimate of how long the project will take will nearly always become the reality.

For projects with high levels of uncertainty, agile is the best approach when planning for change for the following reasons:

- It is focused more on planning than on the plan.
- It embraces and creates a culture of consistent change.
- It creates a culture where plans change.

This doesn't mean that the product owner doesn't have a clue what is happening from one day to the next. Instead, it means that the product owner knows with a good degree of certainty what will happen in the near future and has a good idea what will happen in the medium term, but also knows that longer-term plans come with more risk and uncertainty.

The agile approach leads to an efficient team that not only works to the healthy maximum of its resources, but also increases its productivity as the team develops.

The Five Themes of Agile Software Development

I n the book *The Art of Agile Software Development,* James Shore outlines five broad themes that agile software-development work falls into.

1. Improve the Process

There is a broad and evolving mass of material in the body of knowledge that is agile project management. This area is especially useful for complex projects such as software-development projects, and this industry has always been changing quickly and applying new models and techniques to the new landscape.

Therefore, it makes sense that the agile management process itself should be "agile" and changeable and evolve over time as the landscape changes

2. Rely on People

Agile project management recognizes that people cannot be plugged in and out of a project without somehow impacting the result. Agile project management is not only about the people; it goes one level higher and says it is about the team. The team is an indivisible group of people that is always greater than the sum of its parts.

From an accountability point of view, the agile method focuses on the team and holds the team accountable. The team makes commitments to complete a certain number of stories. The team endeavors to maintain a stable velocity during a project. The team celebrates the wins and shoulders the losses.

In other businesses, people can be plugged in and out with little impact on the end result. A cashier in a shop can be replaced with someone with similar experience and can still cover the nine-to-five shift just as well. In an agile team, this is not the case. The knowledge, experience, working dynamic, and position on the team cannot be easily replaced.

When a project is going off schedule, management sometimes wonders if throwing more people at the project will get it back on track. Agile project managers know from experience that adding staff to a late project just makes it later. Some things can be done to speed things up slightly, but, in general, you have to trust the people.

3. Eliminate Waste

One of the core principles of agile software management is leaving things to the last responsible moment. This principle shines through in many aspects of a project and gives the best example of how a project managed with an agile approach eliminates waste.

Leaving things to the last responsible moment gives the team an opportunity to have as much information as possible before having to commit to a decision. The last responsible moment is the last point in time a decision can be made without impacting the result. It gives the team as much time as possible to get comfortable with a new technology and with each other before committing to an approach it might regret later. It gives customers as much time as possible to ensure that they are happy with the course the project is going down before they need to commit to certain decisions. It gives time to adjust to market conditions.

In traditional software development, 67 percent of features that are developed are never used. Using an agile method will help bring this figure as low as possible by ensuring that as much information is in place before a final decision is made.

There is a saying in agile software development, "Simplicity is the art of maximizing the work not done." Imagine never using 67 percent of the work a team does. Software developers are expensive. Picture them sitting on their hands or playing computer games for more than half the time. The above saying means an agile approach makes things simple by having a process that ensures that the least amount of work is done to achieve the desired result.

Albert Einstein said, "Everything should be made as simple as possible, but not one bit simpler." There is great skill in knowing what to leave out when completing a task. The different approaches to agile project management present a set of skills and practices that can be learned to improve your ability to keep the product or service you are building as simple as possible and built with the least amount of waste.

4. Deliver Value

Software developers are smart, busy people. Because only software developers understand the code, other people in a business are sometimes intimidated to approach them. Their colleagues may fear they will look stupid if they jump in with a suggestion or a new approach.

The work that the software developers do is important, so how can others in the business step in and interrupt them?

Agile projects fundamentally change this dynamic by always putting the customer at the center of the loop. The fundamental starting point for an agile project is that it is centered on delivering value to the customer. The customer is at the center of everything.

Whether it is writing the project charter, writing user stories, or implementing solutions, the customer is at the center of the loop. This is crucial because at the end of the day, the project is judged by how useful it is to the customer. The code may be written beautifully, be bug free, and have tons of functionality, but if it is not seen as valuable to the customer, it is worthless. The customer must always be central to the process. Everything in the process of completing the project must be approached in such a way that the customer is at the center and feels the ownership of the product or service being created.

5. Seek Technical Excellence

Whether it is the ten-minute build, test-driven development, or pair programming, there are many parts of an agile software project that are just part of the technical process and are never visible to the customer.

These parts are like the components of your car. You may never know exactly how they work, but when you press the accelerator, you'll know if it is a technically excellent BMW or a less-than-brilliant Lada.

There are many techniques in agile project management that can be adopted as the need arises. Not all of them need to be implemented, but adhering to most of them will ensure that your team is a high-performance machine. Trying different things out and seeing what works for your setup is a good process, and staying up-to-date with evolving trends and best practice is recommended.

How the code works under the hood is important, and it is important that the whole team seeks technical excellence and that the project-management methodology ensures that is the case.

The Business Argument for Adopting Agile

Innovation distinguishes between a leader and a follower.
—STEVE JOBS

I f a large business with no history with an agile approach tries to adopt it overnight, it would be a turbulent process.

This is because you need everyone on board to adopt an agile methodology, and all the stakeholders involved in projects need to have a solid understanding of the key concepts. The reason for this is that agile methods are fundamentally different from other, more-established approaches to managing projects, and stakeholders need to understand the differences.

In industry, people talk about concepts such as "lean," "iterations," and "agile," but, in many cases, these are just buzz words that are used in a literal sense to describe something rather than illustrating an understanding of any particular agile methodology.

There are five broad steps to adopting an agile method to managing projects:

5. Have senior management support.
6. Hire a qualified and experienced agile expert.

7. Pick a project team that is willing to try agile and that has a suitable project.
8. Complete a trial project, and share the process and results.
9. If senior management is happy, set up an agile management office (AMO), plan the education of staff, and then roll agile out company wide.

The first part of this puzzle is getting senior management support.

So why should a company explore whether adopting agile methods is suitable for them?

1. Faster Product Adaptability to Market Changes

If the company is in a competitive market, it is important that its products can adapt to changes in the market quickly and that it can seize on new opportunities before the competition. Two key principles of the agile manifesto are

- responding to change over following a plan and
- customer collaboration over contract negotiation.

Agile methods are based on releasing new iterations of the product as quickly and frequently as possible, allowing the company's products to constantly adapt to changes in the market.

The second principle listed above is the emphasis placed on collaborating with customers. This ensures that not only are product releases as frequent as possible, they are also in-line with the changing needs of the customer.

Sounds so simple, but not all approaches are based on such principles.

2. Continuous Innovation

Another two principles of the agile manifesto are

- individuals and interactions over processes and tools and
- working software over comprehensive documentation.

Agile methods are not one-size-fits-all. There are many different types of agile methods, each of which is perfect for a different situation. Each agile approach for a company can be tailored to match the company's specific needs. This doesn't mean that anything goes. You still need an expert agile practitioner to guide you through the process, but it does mean that there is room for continuous innovation even in how the team works.

Working software is fundamental to the success of any agile method. If you are going to release a product at frequent intervals, it must work 100 percent of the time. In each agile method, there are various technical systems in place to ensure that the product works all the time, or, in agile terms, every feature is "done-done" before it is considered finished. Knowing that a new feature will work when it is released makes it much easier to have continuous product innovation.

3. Predictable Results

An established agile project has a tempo like the beating of a drum. Although iteration, epic, and release dates may vary in length, the length for an individual project is consistent.

Iterations will demo new features every two weeks. Epics will demonstrate a theme of features every three iterations, and a release will be made every three epics.

All the released features are done-done, meaning they are completely finished and tested, and all the features have been built with the customer who will use them central to the whole process.

Releases are made frequently, so any mistaken assumption can be quickly rectified after seeing how the market responds to the product.

An agile team's velocity is one of the key indicators of its progress working through a product backlog. This roughly translates into the number of features the team finishes per iteration. There are agile processes that help to ensure that the velocity of a team is as predictable and consistent as possible.

Managers with their fingers on the pulse of an agile project will see consistent results over time.

How Agile Project Management Simplifies the Constraints of Resources/Time/Functionality

P eople who know little about agile project management sometimes say that this way of managing a project is like not managing at all, as the plans seem so threadbare.

They are familiar with detailed project plans that outline exactly who will do what, when, and at what cost and exactly what the end product will look like. Unfortunately, in order for that approach to be used, you must have few variables and have many similar previous experiences to compare to. In software project management, that is not the case.

Then, is it true that the agile method of managing a project is just a matter of throwing the plans out the window? Not at all. It is only that the structures that are common across the different agile approaches to project management don't focus directly on resources, time, and functionality. The focus is, instead, on delivering value to the customer; improving the process, technical excellence, and team; and eliminating waste. The two approaches have fundamentally different focuses.

Time

In an agile approach, progress is measured by the number of user stories a team has implemented. Planning can be done by measuring the team's velocity and using the velocity to estimate how long (time) it will take future user stories to be implemented. The velocity of the team is measured by averaging the number of user stories a team has implemented over all the previous iterations. Managing a project in this way means the "plans" are alive and part of the process. It is based on the team's actual real-time performance, thus making the estimating process more accurate.

Cost and Resources

Often for an agile/scrum team, human resources are set at the beginning. In traditional project management, the plan may specify when you will need a database expert or a front end designer. These plans mean that you need certain things to be finished exactly on time, before the next person can begin work. This method means that you don't have a team working on a project but a group of individuals who sometimes overlap in their work.

In an agile environment, the team is often set from the start. Everyone has the title of engineer, even though they may have specialized skills. If an SQL query needs to be written, the GUI designer might write it, not the database expert, because the database expert might be out that day or busy with something else. Everyone needs to be able to do everyone else's job to some degree. This methodology considerably simplifies the management of resources on a project and strengthens the team ethic. It also results in productive and efficient teams.

Functionality

The functionality in a traditional project is often completely outlined at the start of the project, and the product manager will try to estimate how long and exactly when each feature will be implemented.

In the agile methodology, the process is more dynamic. It takes into account that, in some projects, things change all the time, and the methodology must account for that. At the start of the project, many of the features of the product are specified, with the most important ones prioritized. However, over the course of the project, new features can be added and existing ones reprioritized as new information becomes available. This can result in the end product being very different from the initial idea while being exactly what the product owner wanted.

WHY AGILE? HERE IS HOW 3,925 PROFESSIONALS RESPONDED

If the statistics are boring, then you've got the wrong numbers.
—EDWARD R. TUFTE

Sometimes you have to do things the wrong way to really appreciate doing them the right way. Having worked twenty years in the software industry, I have experienced many different approaches to managing software projects, and the agile approach is the best I have experienced so far.

Agile project management gives me the impression that it was created by people who fully understand the complete process of software development and deployment. They understand how to create software that meets management's objectives, and, most importantly, they understand the customer.

It is a cliché that "the customer is always right," but as long as they are the ones paying the bills and deciding if the software matches their needs or not, then a methodology that puts them at the center of everything is much more likely to be successful than one that doesn't.

Some Have Failed

But not everyone has had success using agile methods to manage their software projects. Version One's annual survey, "State of Agile™

Survey," gives some stark warnings to companies that are thinking of adopting an agile approach and points to opportunities for others in the industry.

The number-one reason companies fail to successfully adopt agile methods to managing software projects is of a lack of experience with the methods. As this method has only started to gain traction in the past decade, it may be hard to find experienced practitioners with good track records. However, insisting on hiring qualified agile project managers will ensure a higher level of success.

The second and third highest reasons for the failure of agile projects can be coupled together. The second is lack of management support, and the third is external pressure to follow traditional practices.

Agile approaches are fundamentally different to traditional practices. The amount of engagement needed by stakeholders is higher. The amount of documentation is less, and the nature of reporting to management is different.

Senior management support for adopting agile methods is fundamental to its success in a company. Not only is senior management's support imperative, they also need to have a thorough understanding of the fundamentals of this project-management methodology. Without a good understanding, when the project comes under pressure, they are likely to want to revert to methods they are comfortable with.

The report also signaled that many organizations were either intentionally or unknowingly not using many of the core aspects of agile project management, such as using a product backlog, daily stand-up meetings, or short iterations. This again points to the lack of qualified agile practitioners in these teams.

The final factor that pointed to the lack of qualified agile practitioners in companies or sufficient buy-in from management is the reporting. Rather than focusing on the value that is created for the customer, the top two factors that were used to measure success were on-time delivery (constraints) and product quality. Having on-time delivery as the top measure of success illustrates that constraints are valued higher than producing value.

An Evolving Industry

The agile project-management movement is still in its infancy when compared to more-established practices. Companies know and understand and have tried and tested other approaches. They know what to expect, but when adopting agile, especially for larger organizations, there are not many who have more than five years' experience.

The survey reports that of the 3,925 respondents, 76 percent are using agile in some form for less than five years. It is likely that even with those who have been using it for longer, they would have started off in a small, controlled way and have grown their agile teams each year.

The most common industries using agile are software development, financial services, professional services, health care, government, and manufacturing.

For those that have started to scale their agile program, they offer the following advice:

- Have consistent processes and practices.
- Ensure you have executive sponsorship.
- Have a common platform across teams.

Results

More than half of respondents said that the majority (if not all) of their projects that used agile methods were successful.

The top benefits reported in the survey were

- ability to manage changing priorities (87 percent);
- increased team productivity (84 percent);

- improved project visibility (82 percent);
- increased team morale/motivation (79 percent);
- better delivery predictability (79 percent);
- enhanced software quality (78 percent);
- faster time to market (77 percent);
- reduced project risk (76 percent);
- improved business/IT alignment (75 percent);
- improved engineering discipline (72 percent);
- enhanced software maintainability (68 percent); and
- better-managed distributed teams (59 percent).

Is Agile for Your Team?

If you have read about agile and think it could help your team build products that serve your customer better, there are two important things to draw from this survey:

- Ensure you have fully qualified and preferably experienced agile project managers leading the team.
- Ensure you have executive management buy-in.

Made in the USA
Columbia, SC
27 March 2018